Praise for *Inside the Minds*

"Need-to-read inside information and analysis that will improve your bottom line—the best source in the business." – Daniel J. Moore, Member, Harris Beach LLP

"The *Inside the Minds* series is a valuable probe into the thoughts, perspectives, and techniques of accomplished professionals…" – Chuck Birenbaum, Partner, Thelen Reid & Priest

"Aspatore has tapped into a goldmine of knowledge and expertise ignored by other publishing houses." – Jack Barsky, Managing Director, Information Technology and CIO, ConEdison Solutions

"Unlike any other publisher—actual authors that are on the front lines of what is happening in industry." – Paul A. Sellers, Executive Director, National Sales, Fleet and Remarketing, Hyundai Motor America

"A snapshot of everything you need…" – Charles Koob, Co-Head of Litigation Department, Simpson Thacher & Bartlet

"Everything good books should be—honest, informative, inspiring, and incredibly well written." – Patti D. Hill, President, BlabberMouth PR

"Great information for both novices and experts." – Patrick Ennis, Partner, ARCH Venture Partners

"A rare peek behind the curtains and into the minds of the industry's best." – Brandon Baum, Partner, Cooley Godward

"Intensely personal, practical advice from seasoned deal-makers." – Mary Ann Jorgenson, Coordinator of Business Practice Area, Squire, Sanders & Dempsey

"Great practical advice and thoughtful insights." – Mark Gruhin, Partner, Schmeltzer, Aptaker & Shepard PC

"Reading about real-world strategies from real working people beats the typical business book hands down." – Andrew Ceccon, CMO, OnlineBenefits Inc.

"Books of this publisher are syntheses of actual experiences of real-life, hands-on, front-line leaders—no academic or theoretical nonsense here. Comprehensive, tightly organized, yet nonetheless motivational!" – Lac V. Tran, Senior Vice President, CIO, and Associate Dean, Rush University Medical Center

"Aspatore is unlike other publishers…books feature cutting-edge information provided by top executives working on the front lines of an industry." – Debra Reisenthel, President and CEO, Novasys Medical Inc.

www.Aspatore.com

Aspatore Books is the largest and most exclusive publisher of C-Level executives (CEO, CFO, CTO, CMO, partner) from the world's most respected companies and law firms. Aspatore annually publishes a select group of C-Level executives from the Global 1,000, top 250 law firms (partners and chairs), and other leading companies of all sizes. C-Level Business Intelligence™, as conceptualized and developed by Aspatore Books, provides professionals of all levels with proven business intelligence from industry insiders—direct and unfiltered insight from those who know it best—as opposed to third-party accounts offered by unknown authors and analysts. Aspatore Books is committed to publishing an innovative line of business and legal books, those which lay forth principles and offer insights that, when employed, can have a direct financial impact on the reader's business objectives, whatever they may be. In essence, Aspatore publishes critical tools—need-to-read as opposed to nice-to-read books—for all business professionals.

Inside the Minds

The critically acclaimed *Inside the Minds* series provides readers of all levels with proven business intelligence from C-Level executives (CEO, CFO, CTO, CMO, partner) from the world's most respected companies. Each chapter is comparable to a white paper or essay and is a future-oriented look at where an industry/profession/topic is heading and the most important issues for future success. Each author has been carefully chosen through an exhaustive selection process by the *Inside the Minds* editorial board to write a chapter for this book. *Inside the Minds* was conceived in order to give readers actual insights into the leading minds of business executives worldwide. Because so few books or other publications are actually written by executives in industry, *Inside the Minds* presents an unprecedented look at various industries and professions never before available.

Business School Leadership Strategies

*Top Deans on Creating a Strategic Vision,
Planning for the Future, and Developing
Leadership in Education*

ASPATORE
BOOKS

BOOK IDEA SUBMISSIONS

If you are a C-Level executive or senior lawyer interested in submitting a book idea or manuscript to the Aspatore editorial board, please e-mail authors@aspatore.com. Aspatore is especially looking for highly specific book ideas that would have a direct financial impact on behalf of a reader. Completed books can range from 20 to 2,000 pages—the topic and "need to read" aspect of the material are most important, not the length. Include your book idea, biography, and any additional pertinent information.

ARTICLE SUBMISSIONS

If you are a C-Level executive or senior lawyer interested in submitting an article idea (or content from an article previously written but never formally published), please e-mail authors@aspatore.com. Aspatore is especially looking for highly specific articles that would be part of our *Executive Reports* series. Completed reports can range from 2 to 20 pages and are distributed as coil-bound reports to bookstores nationwide. Include your article idea, biography, and any additional information.

GIVE A VIDEO LEADERSHIP SEMINAR

If you are interested in giving a Video Leadership Seminar™, please e-mail the ReedLogic speaker board (a partner of Aspatore Books) at speakers@reedlogic.com. If selected, ReedLogic would work with you to identify the topic, create interview questions, and coordinate the filming of the interview. ReedLogic studios then professionally produce the video and turn it into a Video Leadership Seminar™ on your area of expertise. The final product is burned onto DVD and distributed to bookstores nationwide.

Published by Aspatore Inc.

For corrections, company/title updates, comments, or any other inquiries, please e-mail store@aspatore.com.

First Printing, 2006
10 9 8 7 6 5 4 3 2 1

ISBN 1-59622-604-8
Library of Congress Control Number: 2006909322

Inside the Minds Project Manager, Kristen Skarupa; edited by Eddie Fournier; proofread by Megan Chromik

Material in this book is for educational purposes only. This book is sold with the understanding that neither any of the authors nor the publisher are engaged in rendering legal, accounting, investment, or any other professional service. Neither the publisher nor the authors assume any liability for any errors or omissions, or for how this book or its contents are used or interpreted, or for any consequences resulting directly or indirectly from the use of this book. For legal advice or any other, please consult your personal lawyer or the appropriate professional.

The views expressed by the individuals in this book (or the individuals on the cover) do not necessarily reflect the views shared by the companies they are employed by (or the companies mentioned in this book). The employment status and affiliations of authors with the companies referenced are subject to change.

Business School Leadership Strategies

Top Deans on Creating a Strategic Vision, Planning for the Future, and Developing Leadership in Education

CONTENTS

Thoughts on the Process of Becoming a Dean

John T. Wholihan, Ph.D.

Dean, College of Business Administration

Loyola Marymount University

Studying the Job Market

The vast majority of deanships that open each year are not in the most prestigious and ranked schools. Although many of what may be referred to as "tier-two schools" seek experienced deans, the reality is that these schools are often the opportunity for assistant and associate deans to secure their initial deanships. Since the average tenure for a business dean is approximately four years, the churning at these schools should be viewed as a real opportunity for those ready to advance in their administrative careers. The array of schools in this category is diverse, and it includes public and private institutions, religious and non-denominational schools, union and non-union faculty, and single- and multiple-level program schools, undergraduate-only through the doctoral level.

This spectrum of offerings requires potential candidates to think clearly about what they want and are ready to handle. Further, it demands that candidates perform careful due diligence on schools before submitting their credentials. It also demands that the analysis is much broader and deeper than what seems to have become the standard for the ill-prepared applicant: namely, reviewing the university and college Web site and listening to representatives of the often-used search firms deliver their stories. If applicants are not networked to probe below such surface-level analyses, there is a good chance they will be found wanting in the interview process, even if their credentials are sufficient to allow them to advance to an off-site or campus interview.

In the investigation process, potential applicants should make decisions about their "fit" with each school. No one likes rejection, and the shotgun approach to submitting applications for just any deanship will waste time and may result in a steady flow of rejection letters. Although the information on Web sites is valuable, it is insufficient. In the due diligence process, one should consider the information from multiple sources such as the Association for the Advancement of Collegiate Schools of Business International (AACSB), regional accrediting organizations, and professional organizations. The informal network of deans and associate deans contains the answers to the less obvious and often disturbing issues. Do not even consider a campus interview without completing a thorough analysis of each school.

Preparing for Negotiations and Future Complications

Prior to and during your due diligence of the schools, a clear understanding of the requirements to support your family is critical. Employment of a spouse, school changes for children, weather conditions, medical care, and distance from aging parents are just a few of the issues of concern. Two professionals without children living separately may work, but it may also endanger a marriage. Clarity on these issues is critical before accepting a deanship, because a new dean is expected to "hit the ground running."

Success in being selected as the dean will prove the extent of your preparation, and this includes the preparation to negotiate for what you want, what the college needs, and what the administration thinks is appropriate. Being offered the deanship is one measure of success. Negotiating the right package for both yourself and the college is the real measure of success, with long-term implications.

Having successfully traversed the path to the new deanship and landed your dream job, you may soon discover that the dream job has elements of a nightmare. The less rigorous your institutional analysis, the greater the likelihood that you will discover some bad dream components. Remember, in the search process, the institution is the seller. They may not want to reveal all of the ills or disadvantages of the job to the candidates. So, the old adage applies, "Buyer beware!"

The issues related to AACSB accreditation or reaffirmation need to be made clear. Any candidate for a deanship should be given the complete file on accreditation. If accreditation is yet to be achieved, has the process been started? Has a consultant been used? Has the college entered into the pre-accreditation stage? If accredited, when is reaffirmation scheduled? What was the content of the most recent reaffirmation letter? Were any specific issues identified requiring interim reports? More than one new dean has been surprised by not asking the questions and verifying the answers about the status of accreditation.

As a new dean, the pressures will be far greater than you expect. Even the experience you gained as an associate dean and by observing your dean does not fully prepare you. The honeymoon is short. Multiple constituents wish you well, while at the same time, they are trying to endear themselves in a manner that will produce a favorable review of their own needs and wants. The unseen members of the various constituent groups are watching. Early decisions have potential long-term implications, and failure to act may be even more dangerous.

Upon arrival, a new dean was focused on the need to internationalize the college in keeping with the goals of the AACSB. The emphasis was to be on faculty development with the expectation that core courses would be upgraded with international content. One program was in place that could be used in the development process. It involved faculty and student international travel in the summer with some expected or hoped-for research output. Unfortunately, it was also perceived by some business and non-business faculty as being a bit of a "boondoggle" for the faculty with emphasis on international travel rather than on research on international business practices. The new dean was being observed by the upper administration, who had been warned about the elements of free international travel for the select business faculty.

The financial implications were examined. The so-called boondoggle costs were actually covered by tuition and fees, so it appeared that the warning to the administration was based more on envy and jealousy than on fact. Modifications to the program were implemented to enhance the real internationalization goals. The program was retained, the voices quieted when the facts were made known, and over time an internationalized faculty built substantial international content into the entire curriculum. Failure to act or to sequence the actions as described would likely have undermined the new dean and slowed progress on the internationalization goals.

It is important to review the words that identify the expectations others will have of you as dean. That range of constituents will challenge you, and you may soon ask yourself, "What will keep me sane and on track?" Fortunately, the answer is relatively simple, in words if not in application. The answer is the integrity of your management and leadership philosophy and the challenges between your beliefs and implementation. Another old adage seems to fit: "Those who know others are learned. Those who know themselves are wise."

More than one new dean has been brought down by early failures on small issues. The tug and pull by constituents with the best of intentions often challenges the integrity that is essential for long-term success.

A new dean was preparing to move to his new institution when a letter arrived from a faculty member extolling the benefits to the college if the dean supported the desperate need for new faculty positions in his discipline. A tone of immediacy permeated the letter, which concluded with what turned out to be a bogus date for budgeting new positions. The letter also indicated that there were serious weaknesses amongst the existing faculty in that discipline.

The dean's response was cordial but firm and honest in explaining that his review of the faculty during the interviews revealed various strengths and weaknesses that would be addressed with the leadership upon arrival. He noted that it would be ill-advised to make decisions or commitments without excessive review in consultation with the leadership of the college. A tone that could be read both as appreciation for enlightenment and scolding for the same was delivered.

The new dean did not reveal this end run attempt, but the perpetrator uncannily bragged about trying to be first in line to benefit from whatever the dean negotiated for the college and, in doing so, undermined her own position.

The dean earned immediate respect for not playing favorites and for trying to establish a level playing field for all of the disciplines in the college.

Key Concepts

During the search process, you asked and were asked many questions. Since you signed the contract, the question in your head has been whether the realities are consistent with what you heard or thought you heard. What are the key words and concepts to review?

The first word is "vision." Deans are supposed to be visionaries. This is part of leadership. Do you really have one? How long before you have to address various groups and lay out your vision? Does your vision fit within the institution's vision? Does the administration want you to have a vision or just a plan?

It is common for vision to be a focal point in starting a new deanship. Strategies evolve and develop from the vision and mission. But deanships are often open because of problems, and while the vision is important, it is possible that deft handling of problems will determine your initial success and whether you will survive and have the opportunity to be a visionary.

My first challenge was to get the M.B.A. program accredited. Under the old rules of the AACSB, the undergraduate program could be accredited, and then within five years the M.B.A. program had to be accredited. No progress had been made, and accreditation took on a "do it or else" status. All of the long-term visionary statements about academic excellence would be meaningless without achieving the project goal of accreditation. The project had many more elements than the AACSB standards. The most important one is always the faculty, which included hiring, refocusing, encouraging, and even discharging. Handling the project components of building a faculty team was a problem to be solved, and from it came not only my vision, but more importantly for the long-term, their vision.

The second word is "resources." Are the resources sufficient to realize your vision? If not, where are they? When can you get them, and how? While "moving to the next level of academic excellence" is a common component of the vision, are the resources available? Clarity on the meaning of the "next level" is most important. Inflated opinions of the capacities of the key players—faculty, students, staff, alumni, and the administration—can lead to unrealistic expectations. Being a visionary does not include being a dreamer.

A new dean at a private institution discovered that the institution had a high discount rate. Financial aid had been increased to extend the diversity on campus, and that goal was being achieved. However, there was no merit scholarship money available. The institution was attracting more and better minority students, but losing other students. The new dean confided in me that he had not asked or been told about the discount rate. Badly performed due diligence, combined with a lack of resources to meet expectations, results in a prescription for disaster.

The third word is "timing." The astute new dean will identify realistic goals that can be achieved and sustained. In doing so, faculty, students, and alumni can begin to see and enjoy their contributions to success. Modest goals that show progress are probably better than lofty goals that have a time horizon that only the youngest faculty members would ever see accomplished and that current students will not have a chance to experience.

In the due diligence process, the accreditation or reaffirmation timetable will be clarified. While the process of preparation can be onerous, it can be a great team-building opportunity. Time it so that it becomes a positive experience; that is, start early enough to avoid a project crunch, but not so early as to ensure project burnout. Look at time as a friend as well. The age of the faculty is a time element. Retirements are both positive and negative. When can new faculty be added?

The fourth word is "ownership." It is easy for a dean to feel a strong ownership of the college. The dean is really a chief executive officer, and chief executive officers should have ownership. But ownership shared is ownership realized. The effective dean builds ownership with the constituents from top to bottom and bottom to top. Who is the management team? Associate and assistant deans? Chairs? Directors? The executive committee? Were they inherited or personally chosen? Do they share your passion and vision, or do they just have a job?

Who are the alumni, and how do they participate in ownership with you? This ownership is more than their degree. It is participation on committees and councils and as mentors, employers, and yes, donors. It has to be built, not simply expected.

How are the students encouraged to share in the ownership of the college? It sounds so simple, but many students are never asked into ownership and graduate without it. Clubs, professional fraternities, program options, teams in competitions, and advisory boards are just some of the ways they reach ownership, which is much different from what I call attending or even participation.

The fifth word is "change." Change is an ally and should be used accordingly. Without it life, work, even pleasure would soon be boring. Embrace change and encourage others to do so, and you will be ready for both the expected and unexpected. In many institutions, the position of dean is changing. As a new dean more than twenty years ago, I was almost forbidden from raising external funds. That function was centralized and focused on the "general fund." Five years ago at a development retreat, the deans were encouraged to spend time on development, perhaps as much as 25 percent of their time. Subsequently, each dean was assigned a director of development, took on a goal for the capital campaign, and was encouraged to think about spending as much as 50 percent of his or her time on development.

The former reporting method in development was at year's end. With a new tracking system in place, monthly reports now provide detail on progress to the dean as well as the central administration. Change has led to significant increases in the cash flow of the college, the flexibility to support the faculty and students, and the initiation of new programs that have evolved from our vision and strategic plan. Change resisted is opportunity lost.

The last word is "success." We all want it. We want it in sips and gulps. We want to bathe in it. It is good. It is motivating. But it is also often fleeting. In fact, the cliché "What have you done for me lately?" probably expresses just how fleeting success can seem to be.

Do not despair! Success is a state of mind, particularly so in education, where bonuses and stock options generally do not exist. Success is in the soul, how you see yourself and convey that self-vision to others. They will assign a degree of success to you not only for specific accomplishments such as new buildings, new programs, or achieving a ranking in a magazine, but also by their perception of the integrity of your management and leadership philosophy. Success is a moral victory built on integrity and implemented daily, usually in undefined and unnoticed ways.

Education is being challenged. Assessment, benchmarking, cost controls, and inflation are just some of those challenges. Little success stories emerge from and through each challenge. Are we teaching effectively? That is, are the students learning? Are the faculty still learning, as expressed by such things as scholarship, technologies, and handling diversity with others? Who is doing a better, faster, more cost-efficient job? Can we do all that and still deliver the service we promise? The answer to every question contains an element of measurable success or failure. But ultimately even the deans with the best ranking are only successful if they have implemented the integrity of their management philosophy.

John T. Wholihan has been dean of the College of Business Administration at Loyola Marymount University since 1984. Prior to coming to L.M.U., his administrative experience included five years as associate dean at Bradley University, also serving several years as director of the M.B.A. program and director of the Small Business Institute. During this period, he also taught in the areas of strategic management and international business. He was a Fulbright Scholar in Brazil in 1976.

In addition to successfully preparing the L.M.U. programs for Association for the Advancement of Collegiate Schools of Business International accreditation, Mr. Wholihan has concentrated on enhancing the international focus of the college. He has involved the college in international programs in St. Gallen, Switzerland; Monaco; Bonn, Germany; Montevideo, Uruguay; Sakhalin Island, Russia; Beijing; and elsewhere. The M.B.A. program has refined its famous comparative management systems program. With Mr. Wholihan's leadership and support, the faculty has developed international reputations in several disciplines including strategic management, marketing, finance, and entrepreneurship. Recently, Mr. Wholihan established the Student Investment Fund, a real money program to teach students about investments and risk analysis. He serves on numerous committees including the university strategic planning council.

From 1993 to 1995, Mr. Wholihan focused on final planning, construction, and occupation of the Conrad N. Hilton Center for Business, the 88,000-square-foot home for the college. It opened in August of 1995 with the official dedication in October. Simultaneously, the Casassa Center for Executive Learning, which occupies the third floor of the building, was launched to meet the increasing demand for special development programs for small- and medium-sized businesses.

Mr. Wholihan prepared for his career with a bachelor's degree from the University of Notre Dame, an M.B.A. from Indiana University, and a Ph.D. from the American University. His works have been published in several journals and texts. He is a member of several academic associations and honor societies including the Academy of Management, Small

Business Institute Directors Association, Beta Gamma Sigma, and Alpha Sigma Nu. He will serve as president of the board of governors of Beta Gamma Sigma during 2006–2008. He served as president of the Western Association of Collegiate Schools of Business. He is past president of the Association of Jesuit Colleges and Universities–Business Deans. He was the founding president of the International Association of Jesuit Business Schools. He is a member of the Rotary Club of Los Angeles, the Financial Executives Institute, and the Jonathan Club.

Mr. Wholihan has served on the board of directors of small companies and currently is on the board of trustees of the Turner Funds. He served as chairman of the board of Notre Dame Academy in Los Angeles.

He and his wife, Marlene, are forty-five years married. Their family includes John Jr., J. David, and K. Elizabeth.

Looking Out for
the Students, the Faculty,
and Everyone Else

Jerry Strawser

Dean and Development Council Chair,

Mays Business School

Texas A&M University

The Role of a Business School Dean

As the dean of a business school, I work closely with and for many different audiences, all of whom are integral members of our academic community. These individuals include current and prospective students and their parents, faculty and staff colleagues, university administrators, deans of other colleges, trustees, and many other individuals who are part of our campus family. For students and parents, my role is to ensure that we deliver a high-caliber education while preparing students for careers and providing them with an understanding for the necessity of life-long learning. In order to achieve this goal, I work closely with our faculty and department heads to attract and retain dedicated, passionate, and highly skilled faculty. Once part of our school's community, my responsibility to faculty is to provide them with the appropriate opportunities and incentives to enhance the quality of the education they provide to our students. It is also important that I provide them with the time and resources necessary to allow them to expand knowledge through research in their respective disciplines.

Because of the highly competitive nature of business schools in today's world, deans are more involved than ever in the recruitment of students in all programs (undergraduate, master's, M.B.A., and doctoral). While the size of our school does not provide me with time to meet with every prospective student, I do try to personally meet or speak with our top applicants. The purpose of these meetings is to discuss the students' goals and objectives and evaluate whether we have a mutually beneficial "fit."

In assessing the role of a business school dean in today's academic environment, one cannot ignore the university community and students enrolled in other colleges of study. More students outside of the business school seek some level of business education, whether a basic accounting or finance class or a general survey course in business. Many of these students plan to own or operate their own business at some point in the future and believe basic education in business will be useful to them. As a result, minor areas of study in business are becoming popular and provide another group of constituents for business school deans.

A Dean's Vision: The Fundamental Purpose of a Business School

The overarching purpose of a business school is to influence the manner in which organizations operate and business is conducted. One manner in which we do this is by providing a business education and instilling important values in our students. We educate students to be the next generation of leaders, leaders who will question the status quo and operate with the highest level of integrity. In addition, we also stress and instill the value of serving others in a business environment. Our goal is for our graduates to be outstanding businesspeople and, more importantly, outstanding people.

Business schools also influence the conduct of business by providing an environment in which faculty can challenge current practices, investigate phenomena, and prescribe future practices through their research. To succeed, business schools need to be relevant. We do not have the luxury of the "ivory tower." Because our students must be able to quickly assume responsibilities within organizations that hire them, we must provide relevant education to working professionals. Our faculty's research must investigate important issues and produce results and skills our graduating students can readily implement in their jobs.

My personal goals for my school are to provide significant career and post-baccalaureate education opportunities for our students and professional development and growth opportunities for our faculty. As a professional school, we are more focused on career opportunities and job placements compared to the institution as a whole.

Management in the Education Field

The management process in academe does not differ materially from a managerial role in any other field. Management, regardless of the industry or organization, is about establishing a vision and goals for the organization; motivating and rewarding people for desired behavior consistent with the organization's goals; measuring and evaluating progress toward the organization's goals; and taking actions to continue progress toward these goals. While the goals are obviously different in academe (for example, universities and business schools do not worry about meeting analysts' earnings estimates), the management process is quite similar.

An important part of the management process is related to an organization's greatest asset: its people. As with any organization, it is critical to identify an individual's strengths and put them in a position to use those strengths. Deans must place a tremendous amount of importance on the continued development of faculty and staff colleagues and the understanding that we will all learn something new each and every day. This is not only true for academe but for all industries.

Like all managers, my ability to succeed depends heavily on the quality of my leadership team and faculty and staff colleagues. When seeking out members of our team, I look for people who will question every decision I make, analyze alternatives, and let me know when they disagree with me. They must also understand the importance of faculty and staff life and be able to understand how to motivate faculty and staff. Other attributes that are important for faculty and staff colleagues are creativity, innovation, and the desire to improve each of our programs every single year.

When recruiting faculty and staff, we look for two main attributes: talent and fit. I have seen a number of situations at other institutions where highly talented individuals were hired, but their goals and priorities were not consistent with those of the business school. While hiring a star faculty member creates a sensation in the academy, if that faculty member does not enjoy interacting with students, working as part of a faculty team, mentoring junior faculty, or developing doctoral students, the relationship will not work. While individual stars can exist in some organizational settings, this concept does not work well in an academic setting.

The Most Challenging Aspects of Being a Dean for a Business School

There are many challenges inherent to the role of business school dean. The market for top-quality faculty and top graduate students (M.B.A. students in particular) is quite competitive among business schools. Faculty salaries are often the highest at the university level, which can create a challenge when hiring an entry-level faculty member for a higher salary than a senior professor in another college. Another challenge is that the primary recognition business schools receive through the media is related to the quality of their M.B.A. programs. However, at a university like ours, the M.B.A. program is a very small fraction of our total student population.

The benchmarks I use to measure the success of our institution are:

- Student employment and graduate school opportunities
- Faculty research and its impact on business and academic communities
- Faculty teaching and pedagogical innovations to create a challenging learning experience for our students
- Faculty leadership positions in academic organizations and learned societies

I do not depend heavily on external rankings to judge my own staff's performance, but they are important to many prospective students, employees, and potential employers of our graduates. While they are not perfect by any measure, they are often the most prominent piece of information about a business school, and rankings do influence the choices of students, faculty, and recruiting organizations. One benefit of the rankings is that they provide data against which we can benchmark our performance (qualifications of incoming students, placement results for graduating students, etc.).

I work with our communications staff to ensure that relevant information related to media rankings is disseminated to our constituents. With respect to communicating information on rankings, the most important point is to ensure that our constituents know how the rankings are determined and what they tell us (either good or bad) about our performance. As one example, for the past three years, the percentage of our M.B.A. students employed following graduation has been among the best in the world; clearly, it is important that our constituents are aware of our success in this regard.

Qualities of a Dean: Achieving Long-Term Success

The most important quality for a successful dean, or perhaps for achieving success in any role in the academic field, is patience. While improvements can happen on a day-to-day basis, it is often difficult to see major changes in a short period of time. It is critical to understand that incremental improvements in the short term lead to significant enhancements in the long term. Along the same lines, it is critical that a dean possess a long-term perspective. The average business dean's tenure is less than five years. As a result, initiatives that are undertaken today will often bear fruit under another individual's leadership. If a dean is only interested in doing things that will be completed during his or her term, there will be a great deal of frustration and very little progress.

Many misconceptions exist about deans of business schools. One is that research is of lesser importance for us than it is for deans at schools receiving federal research support, such as schools focusing on engineering and sciences. In fact, business research has resulted in major changes in how companies operate, what information companies are required to disclose in their financial statements, how companies are valued in the equity markets, how companies market their products and services to customers, and many other areas. These changes have significant impacts on our economy and have been influenced by business research.

It is true that we face many challenges in this role. Personnel decisions are always difficult. We have a large number of outstanding faculty; in fact, we have more than we can reward in a meaningful way through our salary and salary raise structure. To be successful, we must focus our rewards on faculty members who have the greatest impact and resist the temptation of "averaging" new funds and distributing them evenly to all of our outstanding faculty. In a sense, this is just like an organization evaluating several competing investment opportunities and making a choice from among these alternatives.

Decanal colleagues at other business schools are an important resource for any business school dean. We are all facing many of the same challenges and issues; in addition, we depend on each other for ideas and best practices. While it is a competitive environment, I have always found that other deans have been quite generous with respect to sharing their time and ideas. Just as one example, when I was dean at the University of Houston, we were in the planning stages of creating a financial trading room; a number of other deans hosted my colleagues and me at their institutions. At

Texas A&M University, we have returned the favor by hosting a number of schools in our Reliant Energy Commodities and Securities Trading Center.

Strategies for a Successful Dean

I believe the strategies of any successful dean must be based on open communication, both internally and externally. Our office frequently communicates information about our school's accomplishments and goals to all of our constituents. We produce hard-copy publications and a monthly electronic newsletter, which are distributed to faculty, staff, current students, former students, university officials, and many other groups. Our goal is to keep people informed about our school and how they can partner with us. For our donors, our communications must provide them with a picture of the current standing of the school, a vision of where we would like the school to move toward, and a summary of how their support can help. It is critical that these communications clearly summarize the priorities of our school.

A popular new addition to our communications portfolio is a weekly electronic newsletter that is sent to all faculty and staff every Monday morning. This allows us to recognize important achievements by our colleagues in a very timely fashion and inform our colleagues about visiting executives and other important events during the upcoming week.

In addition to "telling," communication also requires "listening." I frequently meet with students and recent graduates and make a point of truly listening to them. They are often in the best position to tell me what the competition is doing and the comparative strengths and advantages of our program. One of the greatest advantages of teaching a freshman class (which I do) is that I have a chance to learn about our programs through the eyes of an eighteen-year-old. These individuals are in the best position to answer an important question: why did you choose Texas A&M University (and Mays Business School)? Because of this first-hand interaction with students, we have implemented some changes in our recruiting process that have resulted in significant improvements.

With respect to faculty and staff, when I first assumed this position, I met with them in small groups and asked them to identify three things they would do in my position. I believe we realized several benefits from these meetings. First, and most obviously, it gave me an opportunity to get to know them. Second, it gave them an opportunity to know one another (we arranged these meetings so that no more than a few people from one department could attend the same small group meeting). Finally, the communication during these meetings gave me a very good idea about how everybody felt we could make the most immediate and influential improvements. While several of these suggestions were related to specific programs and initiatives, one was more of a cultural suggestion; based on this suggestion, we hold monthly breakfasts for the entire faculty and staff as a way to encourage them to get to know one another and to begin working more effectively across departments.

One group of faculty I make a special effort to communicate with is untenured faculty. I meet each year with every untenured faculty member to review their progress during the year, evaluate their overall record and accomplishments, and ask how our office can be of assistance to them. The purpose of these meetings is to allow them to succeed: when they assemble their dossier for their tenure case, I want to be sure they are aware of my perspective in their case and that we've done everything we can to provide them with an opportunity to succeed.

The bottom line on communications is that it must be a two-way street: telling and listening. There is a growing tendency toward surveying hundreds and hundreds of graduates, prospective students, employers, deans, faculty, and other groups to try to learn about a school. I believe more can be learned in individual or small group meetings by asking some very simple questions and requesting honest answers in return.

Changes in the Industry: Past, Present, and Future

While business education changes constantly, the biggest current change in our industry is the evolving nature of M.B.A. programs. These programs are heavily influenced by the nature of the economy and have seen major peaks and valleys since the year 2000. In the late 1990s, the economy was booming and the biggest challenge facing M.B.A. students was which offer to select; a few years later, the average employment rate of M.B.A. students hovered around 60 percent, and salaries had declined dramatically. These market conditions led to dramatic shifts in enrollments, and many top programs were admitting students who would not have been competitive in past years.

In the coming years, the demand for and perceived value of the M.B.A. degree is a significant unknown. For private schools, where the M.B.A. program is often the primary (if not sole) generator of revenue, this will have a material impact. Schools such as ours (a public institution with a large undergraduate program) will not be as affected by these market conditions. However, we will need to continue to differentiate our M.B.A. program from competing programs and provide outstanding customer service and value to compete in this marketplace.

Another major change is the market for faculty "stars." Business school faculty markets have evolved into a two-tier market: exceptional faculty and others. Exceptional faculty commands a significant salary premium and compensation package that has widened within the last five years. While these individuals create extraordinary research and teaching programs within their schools, the fact of the matter is that fewer and fewer schools will be able to compete for their talent because of resource constraints.

Within this industry, the role of dean has evolved from an insular, internal role to a far more external role that involves alumni relations, communications, and fundraising. I am confident that this evolution will continue in the coming years.

The Golden Rules

In this role, there are some basic golden rules that will enhance your ability to do your job well. First of all, make the effort to reach out and listen to recent graduates. They work alongside graduates of other institutions and can let you know what your program did well and where it can improve. In my opinion, this is the best way to improve programs. We have created an advisory board of recent graduates; the purpose of this board is not to raise money but to discuss how to improve our programs. Second, a dean should never lose his or her personal touch. Faculty and staff enjoy receiving handwritten notes congratulating them for their successes or thanking them for extraordinary efforts and achievements. This is a gesture that does not take significant time but yields significant benefits. Third, put a strong leadership team in place and let it do its work. Do not do it for them or micromanage them. You need their independent ideas. Finally, develop a network of other deans to discuss ideas and issues with. They are facing many of the same challenges as you: communicating with them will inspire you to think of new ideas, learn of emerging issues, and hone ideas and processes with people who are familiar with the challenges and rewards of the industry.

The best piece of advice I have ever received with respect to heading a business school is that it is absolutely critical to get input. However, in the end, you are responsible for making what you feel is the best decision for the institution. This decision cannot be based on a "vote" or popularity contest; it needs to be right for the institution.

Making Money: How to Bring in Revenue

State institutions operate differently from private institutions in that the major funding for activities (both state-appropriated funding and tuition and fees) is not provided directly to the units (colleges) providing the education but to the university (which then allocates funding across colleges and other support units). As a result, when we admit an additional student, we often do not see any direct financial impact; however, we need to provide instruction, computer support, advising services, and career services to that individual. Because of this funding mechanism, public business schools have needed to be entrepreneurial in the revenue generation process.

Executive education is becoming a more important part of our overall funding strategy. We currently offer both an executive M.B.A. degree, as well as executive (non-degree) programs. Not only do these programs provide significant funding for our activities, but they also provide our faculty with important exposure to managers in a classroom setting. This creates a real two-way learning experience where the managers learn from our faculty and our faculty learns from managers.

In addition to executive education revenue, donations and earnings from endowments are becoming a much more significant factor in our ability to attain excellence. Conceptually, we like to think of our donors providing the "margin of excellence" through gifts of scholarships, program support, and endowed faculty positions that allow us to attract outstanding people. In a sense, we view the budget allocation from the university as providing a basic level of service and the revenues from executive education and donors as allowing us to move toward a premium level of service.

The most expensive elements of operating a business school include payroll, particularly faculty salaries, and stipends and scholarships to attract top graduate students. Another significant expense is the investment made in facilities and technology. While technology and online learning has a powerful impact on education, I do not believe it will replace face-to-face education in any significant way. I do believe it will allow faculty to spend their classroom time more productively and use technology to handle the more mundane and basic matters in their classes.

Determining the Cost of Tuition

In the past five years, increases in the cost of a college education have been noted and discussed in the popular media. This issue becomes particularly controversial for public institutions, since they receive funding from the states in which they are domiciled and are perceived by the public to "owe" an affordable education to its citizens. However, the state funding provided to many institutions has declined drastically in recent years, resulting in students and their families having to bear a greater burden of the costs of education. However, when compared with private institutions, the cost of an education at many public institutions is one of the best investments a family can make.

In recent years, many public institutions are moving toward "market-based" tuition for professional schools such as business, engineering, and architecture. Like any business, we operate in a market; we have a demand for our product, we add value to our students, and we provide them with a significant return on their investment upon graduation (in terms of employment in a professional career). Just as an example, we have three times the number of qualified applicants at the undergraduate level as we can admit. In addition, upon graduation, our students will be in a position to begin their careers with leading organizations at an extraordinary salary.

Certainly, we would be wise to price our education considering these market conditions and dwindling state support.

Despite this compelling case, there are other factors to consider. Higher tuition levels for different degree programs introduce the risk of cost (and affordability) playing a significant role in a student's decision as to their desired course of study. This is why financial support (through university financial aid and donor-provided scholarships) assumes additional levels of importance. At public institutions, tuition is a very sensitive issue. On one hand, part of our mission as a state institution is to be affordable and provide education to citizens of the state of Texas. On the other, it is very expensive to operate a top-quality business school, and any improvements we make have significant benefits to our graduates. The dilemma becomes the following: if charging additional tuition provides improvements for the quality of a business school, and these improvements provide more and better job opportunities for our graduates, higher tuition is a good business decision—if these benefits are not realized, it is not.

Building Endowments

Fundraising is absolutely critical to the success—and survival—of our school. Once again, if the major sources of funding are state appropriations, student tuition and fees, executive education revenues, and gifts and earnings from endowments, as some of these sources are reduced, others must be increased just to maintain current levels of operations. Donors need to be informed, and it is important for them to hear where the school is currently situated, where the school needs to go, and how their gifts can help the school achieve its goals.

While fundraising for facilities (buildings, expansions, technology, etc.) provides a very visible and tangible outcome to the donor, it is just as important that fundraising occur for the true assets of a business school: its people. In this process, we communicate to our donors the importance of recruiting outstanding faculty and students to our school and how doing so raises the quality of our school and, in many cases, the value of their own degree. From a financial standpoint, a successful institution must support its very best people—whether faculty, staff, or students—in building great programs. These great programs then provide opportunities for students.

Endowment is built through targeted fundraising efforts geared toward significant donors. In some cases, these efforts involve a group of people (for example, employees of an organization or members of a particular alumni class). In others, they involve a single person or family. Regardless of the type of donor, the fundraising process involves a great deal of communication and interaction, which is appropriate when an individual or group is being asked to make a major financial commitment. Each process is different, but in the end, the funds are deployed based on the wishes of the donor; they could be targeted to support a faculty member, student, or specific program. Endowments must support sustained excellence. Endowments cannot be viewed as substitutes for operating money or state support. They must supplement these funds to improve the quality of our people and programs.

The Popularity of an Institution: Driving Factors

The dean must position the institution to thrive on change in the marketplace. As has been said numerous times, the only constant is change; nothing can be truer in an industry when you have four years to prepare students for a forty-year career. A school cannot do this unless it has innovative faculty whose efforts are fully supported by their colleagues; at our institution, we are fortunate to have this mechanism in place.

Factors driving a school's reputation depend on the audience you are considering. For example, faculty members are influenced by the quality of faculty we have and the support we provide for their work. Outstanding faculty we are recruiting want to work with our current outstanding faculty. Prospective faculty will evaluate our strength in their areas of interest to ensure that we have both people and financial resources that can allow them to continue their work. They also want to have the opportunity to work with outstanding students in programs that are complementary to their areas of research.

On the other hand, our students are heavily influenced by our programs and how these programs will affect their abilities to gain employment with a top organization or admission to a top graduate school. I think business students tend to be more outcome-focused than other students; they ask very pointed questions about which companies recruit our students and where our students obtain employment after graduation.

Jerry Strawser is currently dean of Mays Business School at Texas A&M University. In addition, he holds the development council chair of business and the Leland/Weike chair in accounting. Prior to his appointment at Texas A&M University, Professor Strawser served as interim dean of the C.T. Bauer College of Business at the University of Houston and Arthur Andersen & Co. alumni professor of accounting.

Professor Strawser has co-authored three textbooks and more than sixty journal articles. His research has appeared in such journals as Accounting Horizons, Auditing: A Journal of Practice and Theory, Behavioral Research in Accounting, Journal of Accounting Auditing and Finance, Journal of Accounting Literature, *and* Journal of Accounting Research. *He has also presented more than thirty papers at national academic conferences. In addition to his academic experience, Professor Strawser had prior public accounting experience at two international accounting firms. He has also developed and delivered numerous executive development programs to organizations such as Continental Airlines, ConocoPhillips, Halliburton, KPMG, Minute Maid, PricewaterhouseCoopers, McDermott International, Shell, Southwest Bank of Texas, and the Texas Society of Certified Public Accountants.*

Professor Strawser is a certified public accountant in the state of Texas and earned his B.B.A. and Ph.D. in accounting from Texas A&M University. In addition, he currently serves on the major case enforcement committee of the Texas State Board of Public Accountancy.

Earning a Reputation as a Center of Intellectual Growth

Dr. William A. Dempsey

Dean, College of Business and Economics

Radford University

The Role of a Dean

The overarching role of the dean is to assist the university in achieving its strategic and tactical goals. The dean realizes this goal by participating with other university leaders in the initial process of establishing the university goals and then specifically setting and achieving goals for the business school that are in consonance with the university's mission and objectives.

The dean is responsible to the current and prospective students and their families for providing the best education possible with the available resources. In addition, the dean is responsible to the students, faculty, and staff for acquiring better resources in pursuit of improved faculty teaching and development and, in turn, student learning. The dean must be a leader in engendering and requiring improvements over time in faculty and student scholarship.

The dean is also responsible for fostering a common sense of direction, proper alignment of goals and outcomes, and rewarding achievement in an open, ethical, and professional work environment. It is important that the dean become known for being objective, fair, and consistent in making recommendations and decisions. Making the right decisions in difficult situations is essential. In this vein, it is more important to be respected by most colleagues than it is to be liked by all.

The dean must be the business school's champion when competing for limited resources with other deans and other unit heads. However, the dean must balance the needs of the business school with the needs of other schools and entities within the university in seeking what is best for the university as a whole.

The dean is the personal representative of the school to the outside world including families of students, employers of the school's graduates, alumni, the local community, professional and scholarly associations, government officials, and others who impact or are impacted by the university. Therefore, the dean must be professional in his or her interactions with a variety of constituencies. Doing the above well will fulfill the dean's responsibilities to the trustees, especially in regard to doing what is best for the institution as a whole, not just the business school.

The Role of a Dean at a Business School Compared with the Role of Other Deans

In general, the basic roles of deans as described above largely are the same across various programs, schools, and colleges. Role differences between business school deans and deans of undergraduate programs, law schools, and medical schools primarily relate to what is expected of a school in transforming the skills and knowledge of its students as compared with students in other schools; this is also reflected in what is expected of the dean throughout this transformational process. Differences also derive from what is expected of the dean in connection with external stakeholders.

The dean of an undergraduate school, also known at many universities as the dean of arts and sciences, is responsible for assuring that students receive a strong, broad-based, liberal education, one that most students acquire in their first two years at the university through coursework involving mathematics, physical and social sciences, history, English, and the arts and humanities. A solid liberal education is the foundation on which we build upper-level undergraduate curriculums across a wide spectrum of degree programs, including business programs. The liberal education foundation helps the students continue throughout their lifetimes to develop, learn, and become involved and productive members of society. Undergraduate business programs are built upon a liberal education base. Students who have learned in their first two years of university to be more effective in writing, problem solving (using scientific method), and understanding human behavior and other cultures are going to be better prepared to master the skills and knowledge related to managing businesses they acquire in their last two years in a business school. In this respect, the undergraduate school dean and faculty have roles to play that are as important as the business school dean's. Indeed, when business school alumni are asked which skills or areas of knowledge are most important to success in business and which professor had the most profound impact on them in college, they often mention courses and faculty members in the arts and sciences.

Business school deans are usually expected to interact with the business community to obtain feedback on making appropriate curriculum changes, facilitate finding student internships, and promote the school's graduates with respect to obtaining jobs. Business school alumni who have had time to accumulate wealth through their businesses are strong prospects for fundraising. Thus, the business school dean usually plays an important role in cooperation with university advancement and the top administration in raising funds. Undergraduate school deans are also involved in such activities but often to a lesser extent.

Deans of law schools and medical schools are responsible for assuring rigorous, high-quality educations for students who will become licensed professionals in the fields of law and medicine. Success is more measurable for deans of law schools and medical schools in terms of graduates who pass bar exams and medical licensing exams. Generally, more is expected of professional school deans with respect to fundraising.

The Fundamental Purpose of a Business School

The fundamental purpose of a business school is to increase the success rate for individuals who pursue business and management careers, and the productivity and profitability of the organizations they create or in which they work. Only about 25 percent of bachelor's degrees in the United States are in business. Business school graduates have already shown a desire to pursue a career in business, and they have basic skills and knowledge of the functional areas of business and how to manage an enterprise. Business schools produce graduates who need less training than non-business school graduates at the beginning of their careers in business; this makes business school graduates who go into entry-level positions more valuable to the businesses that retain them.

Ideally, a business school should operate as much as possible like a business, meaning the school will have a strategic plan with a mission and objectives. The school should carry out programs that produce high-quality results in line with student needs and needs of businesses. Finally, the school should improve over time in the face of competition.

School Goals: Declaring and Supporting a Mission Statement

The fundamental goal of my school is to produce graduates capable of effectively competing with graduates from any other business school in the world. Our goals are divided and spelled out in terms of student learning goals, the acquisition and use of human, financial, and physical resources, faculty development, program and process improvements, and maintaining accreditations.

With respect to my university, the institution as a whole is a state university that has a mission to improve the well-being of the state, region, and nation. In particular, the business school contributes to the economic development and advancement of the state, region, and nation. Our annual plans are closely tied to our strategic plan and to the mission of the university. We annually evaluate progress toward achieving our strategic plan, and as appropriate, we adjust our strategic plan. These annual and longer-term achievements are reported to the university and the Association for the Advancement of Collegiate Schools of Business International (AACSB). The business school's programs are subject to five-year review cycles within the university and with the peer accreditation association (the AACSB).

The basic theme of our school is to become better, year in and year out. A critical role for the dean is working with the leadership group in the school, including department chairs, program directors, and faculty leaders, to identify a pertinent vision and communicate this to the faculty in the school, the administration of the university, the students, the board of trustees, and the external world, including alumni. It is essential that the school always be striving toward achieving a better future for the student, faculty and staff, and university. A common goal or rallying point is needed so people in the school have a sense of direction, momentum, and the chance to witness improvements over time. People like to be on a winning team.

Working with Others in the Organization

Within the business school, deans work with department chairs, assistant and/or associate deans, secretaries, graduate assistants, faculty committee chairs, and the faculty in general. We also work closely with the directors of each program, such as the M.B.A. program.

A dean who has previously been a faculty member and a department chair before obtaining this position will know a great deal about what is needed to manage a business school effectively. In higher education, there is a faculty culture with its own social norms that is best understood and appreciated through direct experience. A dean can best learn what does and does not motivate a typical faculty member through experience at the department level. Prior chair experience in managing professors and working with students contributes a lot to a dean's knowing how to be an effective administrator and leader at the school level.

Behind an effective dean, there is almost always a proficient administrative assistant, assistant dean, secretary, or combination of such people, and an associate dean working for the dean. An effective assistant is usually someone who is a self-starter, knows how to work with a variety of constituencies, and is good at organizing and supervising events. It is critical that he or she is discreet and essentially a savvy politician. Loyalty to the dean is important, as the assistant must be willing to tell the dean whatever he or she needs to know, regardless of whether this information is positive or negative. The administrative assistant plays a very important role in organizing the dean's schedule and preparing the materials needed by the dean when the dean is going into a meeting with on-campus or off-campus people.

Additionally, good working relationships with department chairs are critical. Well-run departments are essential to a well-managed school. Some chairs are already experienced. Others are newer to their jobs. It is important for deans to help less-experienced department chairs develop as managers and leaders. Even experienced chairs will occasionally need the dean's consultation and advice, and vice versa. Both department chairs and deans work with professors who are extremely intelligent, have free time available, and enjoy job security. Most professors want to be kept informed on matters that affect or will affect them and want to have confidence that the administrators of their institution are going in the right direction. They also want to have a say in all matters that may affect them, but often they do not necessarily want to be directly involved in making a plan work. In this context, chairs and deans are "the man in the middle" with more responsibility than authority in their management roles. Faculty members are similar to independent agents who work with other faculty members and administrators to achieve loosely defined common goals while maintaining their own individuality and autonomy. Indeed, on occasions, deans and chairs feel like they are "trying to herd cats."

The dean's team consists of administrative assistants usually including the assistant to the dean and an executive secretary. In addition to the tasks described above, these assistants help the dean manage his or her time effectively, organize regular and special meetings as needed, organize special events, and work on behalf of the dean in communicating with leaders of student organizations and external business advisory councils. The dean works closely with the associate dean, who typically works on compiling data, data analysis, forecasting demand, and ensuring compliance with accreditation and university standards. The associate dean also substitutes for the dean at meetings on campus when the dean is not available. The associate dean works with department chairs on coordinating academic programming across the school's departments.

The department chairs are also an important part of the dean's team, as they plan and manage the operations of their departments and work much more directly than the dean does with students and faculty members. The dean of a business school frequently works with the M.B.A. director, who manages recruiting and advising M.B.A. students and coordinates course scheduling and teaching assignments with the department chairs.

When comprising a team, the necessary skills a dean should seek include the ability to work well with people and the ability to use analytical techniques that can be applied to budgeting, statistical techniques, and spreadsheets. Another key ability for which to look is the capacity to write succinct, informed, and easily readable reports and memorandums.

Management in the Education Field Compared with Other Industries

Unlike employees in many other fields, professors are generally not primarily driven by the money they earn or the desire to accumulate significant wealth. They are motivated more by intrinsic rewards found in teaching, research, and service within the university, the local community, and the profession or discipline. Full-time faculty members have more freedom in terms of how they perform their duties and allocate their work schedules, and they have less direct supervision. Many professors identify with the profession of teaching and scholarship in their field of study as much or more than they do with their university.

Faculty members who acquire tenure have virtual lifetime job security, barring conviction for criminal acts or gross incompetence. University administrations are leery of trying to dismiss faculty members even for good cause. Such circumstances provide fertile ground for faculty members and groups to challenge other faculty groups and administration with little or no negative consequences to themselves, even though the dispute may become ugly, counterproductive, and demoralizing. In the corporate world, the losers in a nasty contest would likely be fired or transferred or otherwise penalized. This is generally not so in academia.

Faculty members are bright and well-educated. They are patient and persevering. Some, maybe most, believe they could do as good or a better job than the dean in administering and leading the school. However, rarely do they want to be the dean, since they would have to give up work they prefer doing in teaching and research, as well as the freedoms they enjoy in their work. At present, they have a great deal of free time to devote to matters of importance to them. In addition, some professors have skeptical views of administrators, considered "the suits" or "the people who do not understand us or who try to micromanage us." It is fair to say that professors are much less likely to defer to the authority of the dean or believe they have less skill or capability than the dean.

Given the relative independence, job security, and autonomy accorded to tenured faculty members, deans have to depend on persuasion and carefully follow established processes as found in faculty handbooks and union contracts. Deans need to get the faculty to focus on and achieve common goals. Deans also need to seek ways to minimize misunderstandings and conflicts within the business school that could become dysfunctional. A premium must be placed on communicating with the other administrators and the faculty. Misunderstandings and disagreements should be identified, clarified, and discussed, and corrective actions should be taken as early as possible. In other words, good communications and adherence to policies and procedures are essential in avoiding misunderstandings and time spent on unnecessary conflicts.

Measuring Success for Your School: Benchmarks and Metrics

Success is ultimately measured by how well the school's graduates do in their careers and businesses after they graduate. In other words, how much additional dollar-valued productivity do they add to the economic well-being of their communities and the country due to the skills and knowledge they gained as college students? This is difficult to estimate; therefore surrogate measures are used, including the percentage of graduates who obtain a job at or soon after graduation, which highly desirable companies hire graduates, the average salaries they earn, and later, how well they are doing at certain points in their careers.

Other measures are used as metrics as well, such as how well students do on examinations like the Educational Testing Service's General Field Test in Business. This is based on the assumption that students who do very well compared with prior students or students at other business schools will likely do well in their careers. However, some of the most successful executives and/or business owners were not the "best" students. When they were students, they may have been involved in running their own businesses or spent a great deal of time working to pay for their college studies. These activities resulted in less-than-the-best academic performance compared with what they could have achieved if they were focusing only on student work.

Business school success is also measured by how well the faculty does in its teaching as rated by students and faculty peers (teaching ratings), how productive the faculty as a whole and individual faculty members are in publishing their research (numbers of publications), and how well the faculty and staff perform in consulting and service to external constituencies (numbers of projects completed and estimates of the value added by the work done).

Strategies of a Business School Dean: Helping the School Grow and Achieve Greater Profit

Business school faculty members' salaries are relatively high within the academic world. However, business faculty members are also very productive as measured in average number of students they teach or business degrees granted per faculty member. In other words, the cost to produce a business degree is relatively low. Business students ordinarily pay the same for the courses they take as other students do at a university. Moreover, most business schools attract a relatively large share of a university's students and, as a result, produce a large portion of the overall revenues. Thus, business schools are usually "cash cows," units that generate surpluses (gross profits) that are used elsewhere in the university to support other programs. Given this fact of life in academe, business deans are often faced with having to develop strategies to control growth while sustaining profits instead of increasing the number of students they serve and profits they generate. Business school deans are encountering a growing shortage of Ph.D.-qualified faculty. This leads to the need to use less-qualified faculty to meet expanding programs or to increase the size of classes taught by the fully qualified faculty members.

Increasing the number of students in a program can be achieved by adding a new specialization or major that will attract additional students. For example, the health care industry is a growth industry that will continue to expand for years to come. Some business schools have done very well by adding a health care management major to their M.B.A. programs. This has significant appeal to students employed in the health care industry because an M.B.A. degree is highly transferable to a variety of other career paths, and it has luster in the health care industry. Hospital systems want more of their managers to understand how to manage hospitals using the skills and knowledge expected in businesses in general. Moreover, the business school will increase its ability to appeal to potential donors and sources of grants.

Another strategy to increase the number of students in a business school is to develop working relationships with community colleges in order to foster the transfer of A.S.- and A.A.S.-degreed students into the school's bachelor's degree program. Community college administrators want to be able to offer their students a smooth pathway to earning a bachelor's degree. Four-year institutions that approach the community colleges in a cooperative manner, develop articulation agreements with them, coordinate the advising done by the faculty and staffs at both institutions, and advertise the existing arrangement will do well because not all other four-year institutions want to accept transfer students from community colleges.

Increasing the quality of the business school's programs, gaining recognition for doing so by gaining accreditation or additional accreditations, and promoting more selectivity in admissions to the program can lead to increased demand and greater profitability. The thrust of the U.S. Marine Corps' former advertising theme that the Marine Corps "only needs a few good men" has appeal in academe. Many prospective students want to be in a selective, challenging program.

There are certain strategies and methodologies I have developed over the years to empower me to achieve and maintain success as a dean. In addition to those strategies already mentioned, methodologies I use on a regular basis include:

- Tying decisions to the school's strategic plan
- Making sure that when you make a controversial decision, you clearly explain why in connection with criteria related to what is best for the institution
- Hiring the best people you can and giving them opportunities to develop
- Avoiding procrastination, especially when it is obvious that you must discontinue or transfer someone—further, do this in accordance with proper procedures
- Understanding that it is the dean who sometimes must make the tough "No" decision that others will not make, even though they know the dean is right

The Most Challenging Aspects of Being a Dean for a Business School

Universities and business schools are labor-intensive. There are always a variety of challenges faced by business school deans, most of which involve the human element. Three examples are described below.

One challenge is the suspicion of and sometimes lack of respect for business schools. This typically stems from the perception in the arts and sciences that business schools are vocational and not truly worthy of being in a university. Ironically, this attitude is sometimes even expressed by faculty members in departments that are no less "vocational" but happen to be housed in arts and sciences colleges. This challenge may also be deeper, because often top administrators, vice presidents, and presidents typically come out of schools of arts and sciences. The concerns about business schools being perceived as vocational can be assuaged by the business school deans letting other deans know about the importance business schools place on a strong liberal education foundation, the provision of business courses that are useful to non-business students, the availability of minors in business, the significant financial contributions business schools make to the university, and the academic standards that must be met to obtain and retain AACSB accreditation.

Another challenge business deans encounter from some faculty members is the belief that the dean is a "shop steward" (i.e., that the dean's role is to promote and protect the interests of the faculty over all others). However, though the faculty is very important to the success of the business school, the dean has multiple roles to play in properly balancing the needs of students, the rest of the university, and the state, in public institutions, with the needs of the business school faculty. The dean needs to clearly communicate his or her responsibilities and commitments to other business school stakeholders. When a recommendation or decision by the dean does not conform to a faculty member's or group's interest, the dean must make sure the reasons behind the action are logical and related to what is best for the school and university.

A third challenge, as mentioned, is the business school typically being a cash cow in universities. It is tempting to "milk" or profit from the cow but not feed it enough to maintain long-term health. It is up to the dean to provide fact-based arguments in support of the business school's maintaining and improving the quality of its programs. For example, increased average class sizes and higher student-to-faculty ratios are indicative of less-than-desirable educational quality. Business school enrollments coupled with accreditation standards provide the basis for making convincing arguments against "milking the cow dry."

Qualities of a Dean: Necessary Attributes for Long-Term Success

Deans need to have thick skin. They are going to be automatically criticized or blamed for problems, many of which are beyond their control. Deans personify the institution. Faculty and staff dissatisfactions, disappointments, and blame will sometimes be placed on the dean, even though the fault lies elsewhere. As Matt Dillon, the fictional U.S. Marshall, was known to say, "It comes with the territory."

A sense of humor is indispensable in reducing tension and providing a sense of proportion. Having a life outside the university is advisable in order to provide a balanced perspective on what is important in life.

Being able to hold one's temper, be as dispassionate as possible in tense situations, and understand the motivations, attitudes, and backgrounds of faculty members and other administrators will help a dean stay out of trouble. Focusing on settling scores is debilitating and wasteful. Rather, being watchful and well-prepared for making arguments is helpful to a dean.

Being able to see both short-term and long-term views of the school and its potential, and communicating these views, is useful. A crucial ability is to attract and retain a competent and loyal leadership group. The dean cannot do it all and must rely on trusted and loyal team members to manage and promote a quality school.

The Most Difficult Situations Facing a Dean of a Business School

The most difficult situations deans face involve making personnel decisions that may end up in internal appeal, complaint, or grievance processes or possibly even lawsuits that might go to trial. Many faculty members belong to one or more groups that are protected under state and federal discrimination laws. People over forty years of age, women, racial and ethnic minorities, and those born in other countries sometimes claim the dean's actions have been based on unfair and illegal discrimination. When the stakes are high, such as in a tenure decision case, appeals, complaints, grievances, and lawsuits are quite possible as either threats or actions. A great deal of trouble, lost time, and heartache can be avoided if the school and university have clearly spelled out processes and written criteria pertinent to the decisions that must be made. The dean must always act in an objective manner and remain consistent with the applications of the criteria to faculty or staff members who are affected by the personnel decisions involved. At the beginning stages of an apparent or actual complaint by an angry faculty or staff member, it is critical that the dean dispassionately, objectively, and forthrightly refute claims of discrimination in writing to the claimant, the academic affairs vice president or provost, and the director of human resources. Not doing so allows the claim of discrimination to gain the illusion of having merit. Later on, the prior documentation will be important to third-party arbitrators.

Hostile environment and sexual harassment charges can be minimized or avoided by written descriptions of and procedures for addressing real or alleged hostile environments and sexual harassment. Alleged existence of a hostile work environment or sexual harassment must be addressed in a timely fashion according to the university's procedures in order to stop such behavior early and avoid a worse situation later.

Unfortunately, having criteria for performance evaluations, promotions, and tenure decisions in place is not enough. Faculty members and administrators are sometimes tempted to ignore or fail to apply the criteria to well-liked faculty members or faculty members who are troublesome. Not sticking to the school's criteria has at least two adverse consequences. First, it leaves the institution and individuals such as deans vulnerable to legitimate claims of discrimination, as discussed above. Second, this behavior renders the criteria meaningless and leads to mediocrity or worse.

Deans will sometimes encounter faculty members or chairs who consciously or unconsciously do not want to hire the best faculty candidates because such candidates would threaten the faculty members' future stature in the department or the new faculty members would increase performance expectations and competition for merit pay increases in the department. Even when the case for hiring a strong candidate is obvious, the dean might be given excuses or bogus reasons such as, "The candidate doesn't match our needs" or "We can't pay a high enough salary to hire the candidate." The school cannot improve if such situations go unchallenged by the dean.

Biggest Misconceptions about the Role of a Business School Dean

Deans and the professors in the dean's school are highly educated and accomplished. The dean is the leader of an elite group of educators.

Therefore, to non-educators, especially those who did not go to college, a dean may mistakenly seem to be all-powerful, without checks and balances to his or her control over the school and its programs and professors. This misunderstanding is the result of children being taught to respect and defer to those who are highly educated. Young people are also taught to value education and those who deliver education, especially in regard to universities, which are at the top of the educational pecking order; this may contribute to the misconception that deans are omniscient and in possession of great power.

Another misconception is that since deans have a great deal of authority in their universities and their schools, they ought to be able to get things done quickly. Yet another misconception is that deans must have a very easy job, since they are the "lead" or "head" faculty member in a school in which professors have free time to do interesting things while being well-paid. This misconception ignores the fact that surveys of college professors show that the typical faculty member reports working fifty to sixty hours a week. The truth is that deans usually put more time into their work and have even less freedom than the instructors.

Keeping Your Edge as a Dean of a Business School

To remain effective as a dean, the dean has to be well-prepared to argue successfully on behalf of the business school. To argue effectively, the dean needs to stay on top of the data related both to the school's operations and to environmental factors and trends. In addition, the dean must be aware of any emerging information or tends within his or her own university. Therefore, it is indispensable for a dean to know how to acquire relevant and timely data, analyze data with cause and effect models using statistics, set budgets accurately using the latest techniques, and use spreadsheets effectively.

A dean must participate in conferences, workshops, and accreditation team visits in order to learn how to improve as a dean. Deans learn a lot from one another with respect to becoming more knowledgeable and skillful in their administrative and leadership work.

Having a competent and cooperative leadership group comprising department chairs, directors, assistants, associate deans, and key senior faculty members is also essential to maintaining an edge. Forming coalitions and alliances within the university, within the deanship profession, and outside the university is imperative. Deans must be able to call upon others for assistance in dealing with unfamiliar problems and in gaining political support to succeed in internal and external contests for resources and power. Alliances involve other administrators and faculty members inside and outside the business school. Also, such alliances include influential people from the business and governmental communities, often in the form of advisory councils. The ultimate resource needed for a dean to be effective is human resources: those people mentioned above coupled with an outstanding faculty.

The Importance of Feedback from Various Constituents

It is of the utmost importance to receive feedback from professors, students, and alumni. Much of the time, the feedback comes to the dean indirectly. That is, it comes through department chairs, faculty committees, individual faculty members, or representatives of the students such as student government officers. Therefore, the accuracy or truthfulness of the information depends on how accurate the information is that the intermediary receives and whether the source is unbiased in communicating the information to the dean. In order to verify this information, experience working with these individuals plus a good knowledge of the people involved and their motivations is essential to the dean when making sense of the information being conveyed.

One basic way to get feedback is through formal processes and procedures such as annual faculty evaluations, promotion and tenure decision processes, surveys of students, reports from other administrators and faculty members, and interviews and meetings with the various stakeholders involved in school processes.

The other basic method for gaining feedback is through informal communications that take place in parking lots, at lunch, at social events, in the hallway, and through gossip in general. Informal communications often provide the timeliest and most insightful information on what is really happening, what surprises to anticipate, what opportunities are arising, and so forth. Of course, deans must be wary of misinformation, political undermining, and other risks of gossip and informal information. Yet it is important for deans to use both formal and informal types of information so that one can serve as a check against the veracity of the other.

Advice with Respect to Heading an Institution

The best advice I have ever received regarding the role of dean is to do your job well and not let yourself get pulled into refuting every untruth, half-truth, or misconception started by someone trying to cause trouble. It is impractical and ineffective to stand in the hallway talking to every passerby, trying to relate your side of the story; there just is not enough time to do so and get your real work done. You have to rely on most people knowing you have integrity and wisdom, making it even more important to establish a reputation for being fair and honest. Also, I clearly remember a well-known dean saying to an audience of deans that you (deans) cannot be effective as a dean if you are not willing to give up being the dean—being afraid to do what is right to hold onto your job will make you ineffective, leading eventually to losing it anyway.

In turn, the advice I find myself most often giving others is to "go by the book," especially regarding important and sensitive personnel matters. Following proper processes and adhering to policies and rules are critical habits to developing as a dean.

Changes to the Role of Dean and the Business Education Industry

Over recent years, the role of the dean has changed significantly. The dean is more the person in the middle than ever before. The distance of the dean from top management (the president's cabinet level) has increased. University or college presidents, as they move more toward external roles of fundraising and politicking, have been hiring additional staff members for the presidents' and vice presidents' offices. As a consequence, deans who used to be included in a president's cabinet are not involved as much today. Meanwhile, the distance of the dean from the faculty has decreased as professors demand and obtain more of a role in governing the institution. What this means for a dean is that his or her authority has diminished, but the dean is still held responsible for outcomes over which he or she has less influence than ever before. Perhaps a good analogy is found in what it is like to be a major league baseball manager today compared with thirty years ago. Owners today tend to be like celebrities who control more of the decision-making at the field level while players with huge salaries also have gained more say in what happens at the playing level.

Today, about 65 to 70 percent of high school graduates go to college compared with the 25 percent that attended in 1960. The typical college student today comes from a wider range of the normal curve. This is not necessarily a negative, but the nature of the student in college today has, in general, affected the levels of expectation and performance in universities. To clarify, in 1960, universities were expanding to meet the demand for a college education. Students who did not perform well for whatever reason failed out of college. Today, universities compete for enrollments. Students tend to act more like consumers entitled to satisfaction on their terms today. Grade inflation has evolved, and lower work and performance expectations have taken hold.

Another change is that over the past years, state and federal governments have been imposing standards of learning on school systems to assure the public that students are learning what they should as shown in direct measures; this is done in the form of standardized tests. Assurance of learning has reached into higher education through accreditation standards and the threat of applying standards of learning to higher education.

Teaching and learning technologies have also been dramatically changing, as seen in online degree programs and the emergence of non-traditional institutions such as the University of Phoenix, tablet PCs, powerful and generally available software like Microsoft Office, substantial use of the Internet, and other developments. To a large extent, it is not a matter of the new technologies replacing the old ones but rather a synthesis of the old and new technologies into hybrid delivery systems. For example, a standard lecture class is now frequently supplemented by materials and tutorials via Internet connections supported by sophisticated software applications.

In the near future, deans will be expected more and more to have roles involving external activities including fundraising, grant solicitation, personal promotion of the university and school to employers and prospective students, finding internships for current students, engaging in accreditation work, and other matters. In the industry as a whole, changes will include improvement to the quality of the school's programs and marketing in an increasingly competitive market.

Golden Rules of Being a Business School Dean

Each business school has its own culture, and each dean has his or her unique strategies to handle the challenge of these roles. Nevertheless, despite the diverse challenges and roles of business school deans across the country, there are certain basic rules that will serve any dean well, regardless of circumstances. The first is to understand that faculty peer pressure is the true regulatory force over faculty performance; therefore the dean must be committed to encouraging faculty involvement in setting common goals, performance standards, and performance evaluations. Secondly, a dean should always avoid being petty, a crucial component of maintaining objectivity and professionalism in the role as a dean. Further, a dean should not be afraid to speak up: in this role, you are expected to be a leader. Finally, if you make a mistake, acknowledge it, set it straight, and move on.

Being Both a Center for Intellectual Growth and a Profitable Institution

The best way to strike a balance between truly establishing your school as a center for intellectual growth and functioning as a profitable institution is to become known for having high standards. Follow through on assuring that the standards are met, and promote the performance of your students and faculty. It is critical to find ways to differentiate your programs. Prospective students and faculty members want to be at a university and school that has a reputation for having impressive, solid programs that position them as centers of intellectual growth. Some degree of exclusivity attracts students and faculty members. Because intellectual growth and reputation attract students and faculty, being a center for academic growth and functioning as a profitable organization are not mutually exclusive.

Business schools generate money and make positive financial contributions to the university because they usually attract a sizeable portion of the students at the university, thus generating a significant amount of the university's revenues. At the same time, the cost of operating a business school per degree granted or credit hour produced is medium to low compared with other schools in the university.

Unlike other schools and programs such as engineering, the sciences, and schools of education, business schools do not usually draw substantial grant-related funding. The most significant revenue streams originally come from gifts, particularly from very successful alumni who name buildings, programs, and perhaps even the school. Once a substantial gift is obtained to start a named institute or center, such a center may generate revenue streams through training programs such as certificate programs, or through having a noteworthy, well-funded degree program niche that draws additional students, perhaps at a premium tuition level. An example of this would be an executive M.B.A. program with a strong reputation.

In terms of expenses, higher education is a labor-intensive enterprise. Salaries and benefits typically consume 80 to 90 percent of the operating costs of a school.

Determining Tuition: Factors to Consider

Rising costs drive up tuition. Additionally, declining enrollment puts pressure on the institution to increase tuition since, while certain costs and expenses may be reduced, many costs, such as salaries and benefits of tenured faculty, are fixed and cannot be adjusted. Finally, politics can affect tuition at public universities.

More specifically, the factors that drive up the cost of tuitions include rising costs of operation, particularly salaries and costs of benefits. Also, at public institutions, state appropriations are not as generous today in support of universities, a trend that has caused a greater proportion of the revenues to come from tuition in order to cover costs. This was not the case years ago, when state appropriations were larger. Clearly, political decisions on funding higher education affect tuition. State appropriations combined with tuition revenues cover almost all of the operating costs of a public university. If appropriations are reduced or held constant while costs go up, tuition increases would be higher than normal. Moreover, the state government might freeze or even roll back tuition in response to public pressure; this is especially true when the state's economy is doing poorly. It should be noted that private universities also receive some direct and indirect state funding, such as tuition assistance grants for students who wish to attend the private institution.

Tuition decisions at some universities are affected by the tuitions set at other universities. As in business, the reality is that universities are in an oligopoly situation; that is, they have a handful of competitors with which they compete for students in their market. Universities that compete with one another for students are going to watch each others' prices, or tuition; in the same way there are price leaders in business, there are price leaders among universities. The leader, probably the biggest university or the one with the biggest reputation, will set its tuition rate. Others that compete for the same students will then set their tuition by using a similar percentage increase that will preserve the pricing relationship.

Building and Investing Endowments

Endowments are largely built on the generosity of alumni or the families of alumni. Therefore, to obtain large gifts for endowments for scholarships, chairs, centers, programs, buildings, schools, and even universities, there must be a well-managed process over a period of time employed by the school to build endowments systematically. The process involves identifying and tracking alumni, communicating with them about the university and the school, inspiring them to give annual smaller gifts, and encouraging the size of the gifts to increase over the years. The dean's role is also to persuade alumni to buy tickets to events on campus and attend other relevant events, which makes them feel an enduring and active part of the university. It is also effective to encourage alumni to become part of advisory boards. Above all, a dean should determine what truly appeals to potential benefactors with considerable wealth in order to make a meaningful connection with the potential benefactor before appealing for a gift.

Once endowments are established, the money is invested in relatively safe financial vehicles by professional investors. For items such as an endowed scholarship, the principal amount is also invested in relatively safe financial vehicles so the principal stays intact while the scholarship is provided from income from the investment. Normally, some of the income from an endowment fund is reinvested to build the principal in order to offset the effects of inflation. When we receive a large gift for facilities, it goes directly into the cost of the facility. Often, a private gift is used as leverage for obtaining other smaller private gifts, as well as for obtaining public funding for facilities. Part of a gift to build a facility should be put in an endowed maintenance fund for the facility.

In general, the long-term goals for endowments, such as the support of scholarships, attract strong students who contribute to the school's and university's reputations for having a strong student body. Endowments such as endowed chairs or endowed centers are quite useful in attracting and retaining outstanding faculty members. Endowed chairs, centers, special programs, and unique facilities are all part of how universities or schools gain advantage in competitive positioning in the higher education marketplace.

Fundraising: Setting and Executing Goals

Fundraising is of great importance to any academic institution, and it continues to grow in importance due to states not subsidizing higher education as generously as before and the need for additional funding to acquire resources vital for making the university more competitive with other universities. There are limits on how high tuition can go and how much public support the university will obtain. Consequently, the role of fundraising for a dean is currently a significant one.

The dean works directly with the university's fundraising arm, usually known as the advancement or development office. The alumni office is also involved, since most of the fundraising efforts are aimed at alumni. In conjunction with these groups, the dean, as part of the university's fundraising unit, is able to develop a successful fundraising plan through the collective wisdom, planning, and execution of those involved.

Fundraising goals are set based on where the university or school currently stands with respect to fundraising, and the process is quite similar to setting sales goals for a business. To achieve the sales goals, you must know who your current clients, or givers, are, how much they give, and what they are capable of giving. You must also identify additional prospects. To do so, you must have an updated list of alumni, complete with addresses, who have not yet donated to the school. Of utmost importance, you need a strong sales message, such as a message to alumni saying, "Your giving will make a vital difference in helping the school gain accreditation," that will appeal to prospective donors; only then can you effectively ask them to contribute.

The Role of Trustees in the School

In a broad sense, trustees affect financials for the business school by setting tuition and making decisions that affect the school's enrollments, particularly in adding faculty and investing in facilities. Trustees oversee the strategic and operational plans and decisions of the university, and they receive recommendations for tuition increases proposed by the university's top administration. Sometimes the trustees adjust the recommended tuition level up or down. In general, the university's revenues are affected by tuition and enrollment levels. Budget allocations to the business school are mostly dependent on hiring an appropriate number of faculty members to serve student demand as based on enrollments. Student-to-faculty ratios, average class sizes, faculty qualifications, and accreditation standards are criteria used to decide how many faculty members are needed. Thus, a business school's annual budget is largely a function of enrollments in the school.

The financial situation for a business school stems from a two-step process. First, top administration proposes the strategic plans involving financial implications to the trustees for approval. Growth in the school's faculty and staff positions and increases in the costs of resources will affect and increase the school's budget. On the other hand, growth elsewhere in the university may limit the business school's growth. In the end, the manner in which the trustees perceive the reputation, size, and future potential of the business school relative externally to other business schools and internally to other schools or colleges within the university influence their actions with respect to the school. Trustees ultimately will support the business school's growth, advocate maintaining its current size, or consider limiting the school's growth or even reducing its size.

Defining Success from a Financial Standpoint

Leadership is the key to defining the success of a school from a financial standpoint. The scope of a university's mission and, correspondingly, the mission of a business school within the university may be partly defined by the geographic reach of the institution, meaning the area from which the majority of the school's students are drawn. Business schools may be characterized as being local (within the state), regional (within the state and adjacent states), national (country-wide), or international. A business school does not have to be famous or draw a lot of students from other parts of the country. It does, however, have to be strong in the market in which it is competing with other business schools. Attributes of a successful business school include strong recognition, a solid reputation, and stable enrollments relative to competitors in the market it serves. These factors lead to having a good financial situation by sustaining or growing enrollments and being able to increase tuition as needed, acquire and retain quality faculty members, build endowments, and have political muscle sufficient to push forward needed public support.

Factors that Drive the Popularity of an Institution

The reputation of the students who form the student body of a university and in turn a business school has the most to do with a business school's recognition and popularity, assuming popularity is defined as describing a school where students aspire to go. This is reflected in the weight given to average aptitude scores, such as SAT or ACT, and high-score class rankings of entering freshmen by well-known raters of universities and colleges such as *U.S. News and World Report*. Word of mouth is an essential tool to drive institution popularity, as students tend to talk to their friends and family members about the other students at their school and the rigor of the work expected of them to succeed academically. The school's faculty is critical: they guide, motivate, and evaluate student learning. However, though students fundamentally attend college to study under the faculty, their experience at a school is often defined by their interaction with other students with whom they cooperate and compete; it is this dynamic that makes the ultimate difference in driving recognition.

The existing reputation of the school, particularly how well it is already known, is a significant factor determining the recognition and popularity of a school. Well-known brands are easier to sell regardless of whether the brand is a soft drink or a university.

Further, a university's success in intercollegiate athletics ("big-time sports") can make a big difference. One only has to look at the NCAA's Division I basketball tournaments in March each year to see what success in athletics can do for a university such as George Mason University in 2006 or Gonzaga University in the last decade.

Additionally, the school's size and setting are influential to different student segments. I have been dean at a wide range of universities, from local and regional schools to medium-sized schools that have more than 4,000 students but less than 10,000. I have held the role of dean at universities in residential areas considered to be safe and scenic, with student bodies that are in the middle range of average aptitude scores and a reasonable portion of students with a high potential for success in their careers. The keys to the success of a university have had much to do with promoting the attractive features of the university to the market segments that respond well to what is offered.

The Importance of Rankings and Other Distinguishing School Characteristics

Rankings are most important to business schools that have decided to climb the rankings as a measure of their success. You will see such schools in the *BusinessWeek* and *U.S. News and World Report* rankings. For the majority of business schools, rankings are not as important. Of more importance is whether the business school has achieved and maintained accreditation from the AACSB.

Other important distinguishing characteristics include the scope of programs in the arts, physical and social sciences, and professional studies, including business, and the number of degree-granting levels from bachelor's to master's to doctoral programs. Universities that have medical schools and law schools, as well as Ph.D. programs, will also automatically be better known regionally, nationally, and internationally than local liberal arts colleges.

Faculty members who gain favorable publicity by winning research and teaching prizes or by being interviewed often on television about a subject on which they are recognized as an expert helps the reputation of the school. Among academics, recognition is often determined by the number of refereed journal articles and well-known textbooks published by members of a school's faculty.

In order to build upon and publicize these features, deans work with the public relations departments to put out favorable news stories, produce and distribute publications that are sent to other deans, maintain an engaging Web site that is accessed by prospective students and employers of the school's graduates, and reach out to alumni with promotions on the successes of the school.

Strategizing for the Future: Positioning Your School to Thrive on Change

To build a strong foundation and prepare for the future, it is essential to hire and retain the best faculty members you can get. Send them to conferences and reward them for keeping up in their fields as exemplified by presenting research at conferences and publishing in journals. Schools thrive on the creativity and energy of strong faculties and students. They are the people who effect change within the organization. With a powerful and loyal team in place, external variations, such as changing technologies and economic climates, are challenges for which we are prepared and able to meet and overcome.

With respect to developing technology, emerging technologies and online learning have been used to complement and supplement the "old-fashioned" methods of teaching and learning. It is a matter of synthesizing the best parts of the new with the best features of the old. New technologies will make finding a greater amount of diverse information for teaching, research, and learning easier, faster, and more convenient (whenever and wherever it is needed), while direct student/professor human interaction will continue to be essential in providing the guidance, coaching, mentoring, evaluation, motivation, and parenting necessary for transforming young adults into competent early-career professionals.

In such a dynamic environment, it is a perpetual challenge to plan for the future. The way I overcome this obstacle is to continue to get outside the walls of the university in order to see and hear about changes occurring that need to be recognized and incorporated into planning and operating the school.

Dr. William A. Dempsey has been professor of marketing and the dean of the College of Business and Economics at Radford University, a Virginia public university, since June of 1999. Dr. Dempsey was a professor of marketing and dean of the School of Business Administration at Monmouth University, a private non-sectarian institution, in New Jersey from 1989 to 1999. He led Monmouth University to initial accreditation from the Association for the Advancement of Collegiate Schools of Business International in 1999. For the past several years, he has served on that group's accreditation peer review teams.

Prior to becoming a business school dean, from 1974 to 1988, Dr. Dempsey was an assistant and associate professor of marketing at Temple University. He was chair of the department of marketing for seven and a half of those years. Also during his time with Temple University, Dr. Dempsey was a visiting professor in the Graduate School of Engineering at the Federal University of Rio de Janeiro, Brazil, for seventeen months in 1979 and 1980. Dr. Dempsey was an assistant professor of business administration at East Carolina University from 1972 to 1974 and instructor in marketing for three years at the University of Maryland from 1969 to 1972 after being a research assistant from 1967 to 1969. He was a cost analyst for the Ford Motor Company for a year and a half in 1966 and 1967.

Dr. Dempsey's extensive service to the profession includes the following highlights: president of the Mid-Atlantic Association of Colleges of Business Administration in 1995 and 1996 and member of the executive committee from 1992 to 1997; president of the Philadelphia chapter of the American Marketing Association in 1986 and 1987, member of the board from 1984 to 1988, and chair of the Parlin board of governors (national award) from 1986 to 1988; and member of a number of community and church boards. Earlier in his career, Dr. Dempsey published a number of articles in journals and the proceedings of academic conferences.

Dr. Dempsey earned a D.B.A. in 1973 with a major in marketing and an M.B.A. in 1966 from the University of Maryland, and a B.E.S. in 1964 with a major in industrial engineering and operations research from Johns Hopkins University.

Dedication: *In memory of Len Wollack, a good friend and an invaluable associate dean.*

Transforming the Role of Dean: From Caretaker to CEO

Howard Frank

Dean, Robert H. Smith School of Business

University of Maryland

The Fundamental Purpose of a Business School

The purpose of a business school can be divided into three main missions. The first mission is to generate leading research. A business school needs to be on the forefront of creating new knowledge. This is one of the hallmarks of a truly major global business school. A second component of the mission is to create great business leaders who are able to leverage new tools, adapt readily to change, and think on a global level. These are the characteristics that will drive success in today's global, digital economy. Finally, it is essential to offer a return on investment. Each student will have a career that lasts many decades. Business schools need to think in terms of providing students a high return on investment, not just for the initial job upon graduation, but over the course of a career.

Goals of a Business School Dean

Our goal at the Robert H. Smith School of Business, which is the business school component of the University of Maryland, is simple: we strive to be one of the greatest business schools in the world.

The extraordinary technological developments of the last decade are spawning new rules of economic engagement. The fundamentals of business are being transformed in every market, industry, and nation. Those who understand how to create, manage, and leverage assets across organizations without boundaries by using telecommunications and information technology tools are the new barons of industry.

Like businesses, business schools in the new millennium must transform their knowledge, research base, curricula, and modes of delivery. At the Smith School, we are in the midst of this transformation, with a vision of becoming a model for business education and knowledge advancement for the twenty-first century. Only by achieving this goal can we become the next truly great global business school. The realization of this goal will require certain proactive steps, such as generating truly cutting-edge research and creating great business leaders out of our students, who will go on to have fabulous, high-impact careers.

The University of Maryland is a major research university, and its goal is to become one of the top ten public universities in the country; thus, the Smith School's goal of creating one of the truly great global business schools is entirely consistent with and supportive of the university's mission.

In meeting these goals, my reliance on two groups of leadership teams is critical. One group represents the academic side and is made up of department chairs and senior associate deans for academic programs. The other group is what we call our "senior staff," and those are our associate assistant deans and directors. They run most operations and programs in the school. The senior staff members offer the most interesting divergence from traditional academia because at the Smith School, we address the issue of delegation with a parallel senior staff structure. I have built a corporate-like environment within the business school, where talented senior executives who are specialized in their individual areas work in tandem with the academic structure.

In building my team, I look for the same skills that any chief executive officer looks for in a professional commercial organization. I value innovation and good management skills—and the ability to understand how different functions fit together. In particular, I look for active people who don't let institutional barriers stop them from achieving a goal. In academia, you have many institutional barriers. It is also important that staff and faculty at the Smith School be able to work well in teams because we have a strong team-oriented culture.

Managing in the Education Field Compared with Other Industries

Management in the education field is both quite similar and significantly different from management in other industries. The similarities lie within the fundamentals: leadership is leadership, vision is vision, and good management is good management, regardless of the industry in which you are working. A key difference is that within a business school, the primary productive resource, which is the faculty, is quite independent of the institution. By default and by tradition, senior faculty members associate more with the profession than with the institution. Senior faculty members also have tenure, meaning they do not have the traditional kinds of associations and accountability as an employee in a commercial organization.

As a result, senior faculty members are very independent. Good management within a business school necessitates the alignment of the faculty's interests with that of the institution; it also demands the creation and implementation of a model where the faculty is working singly in a distributed fashion toward central goals. As a dean, every management skill you would need in another industry is necessary, but you must overlay these fundamental skills with a whole additional set of constraints and operations.

Managing in a university environment is like being the chief executive officer of a subsidiary of a large organization. In both environments, leaders have many policies that fit within the parent organization, and a leader must figure out how to best meet the organization's goals within that framework.

Measuring Success: Benchmarks for Deans

The process for measuring success is fairly standard throughout the business education industry. All deans use a rather conventional set of objective benchmarks. We examine:

- Research ratings by department and for the school as a whole
- External rankings average for the school, which, while not correlating strongly with quality, does have a fair amount of correlation with outside recognition
- Student completion and job satisfaction
- Student salaries and job histories
- Amount of donations and alumni giving

Obtaining research information is a matter of culling from several available sources. There are various external Web sites that publish the number of publications that appear in top-tier journals by area and by school. I look at this individually for each department and for the school as a whole, and I measure based on our productivity and output on a yearly basis. Each department also has a set of metrics we track to see year-to-year progress.

We look at every ranking, and I use the average across all rankings because you can't look at any one. We look at our averages across all rankings we participate in against all of the other benchmark schools that were used.

The university gives us completion rates, and we track student salaries and job satisfaction by survey for every graduating student. We measure alumni giving by calculating how much they give and commit as a promise to give in the future.

The Most Challenging Aspects of Being a Dean for a Business School

I think the most interesting aspect of being dean is the fact that there literally are not enough hours in the day for the variety of demands on one's time. The dean works with faculty, students, and alumni on a regular basis. He or she externally represents the school. Other roles involve working on both strategy and finance. If you divide up the day with respect to the role and responsibilities of a dean, you will find that deans should be spending 50 percent of their time on each of these areas.

As a result, a dean needs to be satisfied with being able to get involved in everything without getting so immersed that other areas suffer. He or she also needs to be able to build management and administrative mechanisms that encourage the delegation of responsibility and management, much like a conventional commercial organization.

Qualities of a Dean: Achieving Long-Term Success

The most important attributes of any senior executive of a reasonably large organization are health and energy. A hands-on leader needs to be able to run until he or she drops, and then get up and do it again. In this role, if you do not have health, vitality, and a high level of energy, you cannot get the job done.

The ability to develop and execute a vision and the possession of strong communication skills are also critical to the role of dean. Of further importance is having a reasonable set of management skills, which are different from vision and leadership. Ultimately, a dean also will need a degree of luck. Given a choice between being lucky and being smart, I will take luck. You hear the expression, "People make their own luck," and I have found it to be true. Unlucky people are those who fail to see the opportunities that are randomly occurring. Lucky people see them and grasp them. You cannot grasp all of them, and you cannot count on luck being there exactly when you need it, which means you have to work hard in parallel with luck. But if you put yourself in enough opportunities, there will be random opportunities that surface that you can use to your advantage and to the benefit of your school.

Keeping Your Edge as a Dean of a Business School

You keep your edge as dean by being an optimist. If you are a pessimist, you should not be a dean. You also need a clear understanding of finance. You cannot drive the organization without an understanding of financial management. I am a voracious reader, but the chief way I stay sharp is via hands-on interaction with the school's financial management. I also talk to a lot of people and spend equal amounts of time listening.

Part of my strategy is to be informed, and to this end, I always listen to any type of news without "killing the messenger." It is vitally important to be able to understand the reality of a situation, no matter how hard it is. As a leader, you may externally portray the perception that everything is going smoothly, but you must be able to see situations as they really are. You have to talk to the people who know, including students, alumni, and faculty, and be unafraid to get into the trenches with them. You have to listen to and work alongside these people because otherwise you will never understand what is really happening outside your own office.

A dean must also develop certain long-term strategies to achieve success. I am an entrepreneur. This essentially means I like doing things that have not been done before. I am happy when the environment is changing. Therefore, I look at being dean as a wonderful intellectual challenge. Most people do not like managing in academia. In fact, there is a misnomer that the words "management" and "academia" usually do not go together, but I do not agree with this misconception.

Making the Most of Feedback

You have to hear what your managers are saying, but the most valuable feedback comes from your employees. This is not because your managers are not believable, but every manager who works or reports directly to you has a vested interest in looking good, and thus often filters the information that comes through to you.

In order to elicit feedback in a way that is not threatening, you ask questions that are designed to encourage information without putting people on the spot. For example, if I am trying to determine the caliber of faculty, I ask students to name their favorite classes, as well as the best professors they have ever had. I also ask about their least favorite classes. Once I ask enough students, I get a clear picture.

Key Pieces of Advice

The president of a university who had previously been the dean of a business school told me to come see him for some tips when I informed him that I was becoming dean of a business school. He said, "Here's something you should keep in mind. Everybody's going to ask you for money. And here's what you should do when they ask. You should say, 'That's very interesting' as you put your arm around them and walk them to the door. 'Why don't you write it up?'" This is the most memorable advice I have ever gotten.

Virtually no one ever comes back with a write-up. If they do come back, you know they are serious and then you evaluate it because it may be a good idea. It's easy to hit the dean up for money, but it's hard to think strategically and ask: Has this been blessed by the department? Is this part of the strategic plan? What is the school going to gain out of this? What is our return on investment?

There is one thing I believe in totally: there is no such thing as the status quo. If you are not moving up, you are moving down. It's true in everything. If you just stay even, nature will take you down. Your competitors will take you down. Random events will take you down. You must be working as hard as you can to move forward in order to at least break even. That is my advice.

The Role of Dean: Changes in the Past Five Years

The role of a dean has transitioned from the role of caretaker, which it was decades ago, to the role of a chief executive officer.

Why is this? Technology has made online education a viable alternative and has created a competing mechanism for which the traditional university is not necessarily well-structured. For-profit universities such as the University of Phoenix, which operate within a different cost structure, also create a new challenge. More than half of the Smith School's budget goes to research. In the Phoenix-type model, there is no faculty. They are part-time and working for adjunct rates without the cost of supporting an expensive research infrastructure. If you don't think about that, it's going to hurt in the long run.

The educational industry is also changing in remarkable ways. The development of continuous education models, part-time models, online models, and global education are all in process. Business schools are all at the forefront, and the role of dean in the educational business is tied to a marketplace that is changing faster than academia can possibly react to. Academia is a slow-moving, slow-reacting kind of business.

As a result, there are only two viable places to be: the top or the bottom. There's always room for people at the bottom—the low-cost providers. The top will always survive. You have to make a decision of where you want to be. We want to play at the top—thus our quest for greatness. Education is not a static model anymore, so there is only room at the top.

In the coming years, I expect the role of dean to be as dynamic and changeable as in the past but to an even greater extent. A dean will increasingly need to be an entrepreneurial, global manager.

Golden Rules for Business School Deans

The first golden rule of being the dean of a business school is to maintain a good sense of humor. If you do not, you will hate your job and your role will suffer. Second, remain continuously optimistic. Finally, be aggressive. If you are not, you will get run over by everybody in sight. You will get walked over by your faculty, you will be at the mercy of the university, and you will even get run over by the marketplace. A combination of humor, optimism, and proactive behavior is an excellent recipe for success in this role.

Blending Intellectual Growth with Profitability

As a market-driven, commercial manager, I do not believe you can operate without a profitable financial structure. Creating a high-value-generating business school requires financial wherewithal, and this should be the dean's top priority. Once you create a profitable, fast-growth institution, then you can build intellectual growth and capital.

Our most significant revenue streams come from our educational programs and, in particular, from our graduate education: M.B.A., part-time M.B.A., executive M.B.A., and non-degree programs. The most expensive element of operating a business school is payroll. For example, the Smith School's budget this year is roughly $65 million, and our payroll is more than $30 million. The next most expensive element of operating a business school is derived from a group of items that have comparable costs ranging from $2 million to $4 million each annually; this includes running offices such as the M.B.A. office or career management center, developing and maintaining technology, maintaining facilities, and marketing communications.

Determining Tuition

The Smith School is a state school, so undergraduate tuition is set by the university via the board of regents. The board of regents is appointed by the governor and is influenced by the state legislature, so it is as much a political decision as one involving the needs of the university. The business school's graduate tuitions are market-based but must be approved by the regents.

There are various factors that affect tuition, though I have never seen tuition go down. If you look at the costs built into running an institution, faculty salaries have been going up on average of about 4 or 5 percent annually for some time. Other costs that contribute to tuition increases are tied directly to inflation, while others, such as heating and building costs, have increased much faster than inflation. These are the same factors that drive any business's operations.

Building the School's Endowment

The way we build the school's endowment is by asking our alumni to support various projects for the school. The money then goes into an overall university endowment fund and is invested by professional managers. The monies donated for the business school are dedicated to us and can be used only for the purposes for which they were given.

When I first came to the Smith School, we had a $6.5 million endowment. We have had a substantial number of gifts over the last five to seven years totaling approximately $100 million, with close to half going into endowment.

Financial support from our alumni has allowed the school to make a giant leap into a leadership position in the digital economy. The Smith School was named in honor of Robert H. Smith in 1998, when he provided an endowment of $15 million, the school's largest gift ever. Since then, the school's stature and size have undergone a dramatic transformation with the addition of world-class research centers, top-flight faculty, and increased student quality.

You cannot think of managing an endowment in general terms. You have to think in specific terms to meet the agreement between you and the donor and the school.

The Process of Fundraising: Setting Goals and Executing Against Them

Successful fundraising entails thinking in terms of what is truly important strategically for the school. The answer, in general terms, is obvious:

- People
- Facilities
- Wherewithal to deliver first-class education

As far as people, there are two kinds: faculty and students. For faculty, you want endowed positions. For students, you want scholarships. We are also constantly investing in facilities. Since my arrival here, we have built more than $60 million in facilities, and so part of our fundraising goal is to pay for those facilities.

The distribution between these areas is determined by discussions among our senior managers, with the number-one priority given to what we think is realistic to generate in each area and then to what the school's needs are.

Fundraising is essential. If you look at a major public business school, there is no difference between it and a private business school in terms of cost structure. If I am going to compete for faculty, I am going to compete for the best faculty, and these individuals have the choice of going to either a public or private school. We are going to pay them the same as if they went to the top private institution. If I am going to create a building, the fact that it is sitting on University of Maryland ground does not make it any cheaper to build than if it were sitting on Harvard or Wharton ground. Nobody cares about public versus private when we are heating the building.

Thus, if you look at the life of any major school, fundraising is one of the critical ways of achieving goals. There are really only three ways you can get money: you can earn it, you can steal it, or someone can give it you. And since we are not in the business of stealing money, someone must give it to us or we have to earn it. So, how do you go about fundraising? The execution of it is actually quite systematic and sophisticated: it is marketing. You build a marketing plan. You look at who your potential donors are, and then you actually meet with them. You put a marketing organization, which in a university setting is a development organization, in place, and you call on people continuously for years and build individual relationships.

The board of regents has a very significant role. It sets an environment that is even more important than the specific financial role it plays in setting tuition levels. It is a key influencer in how people view public education.

Determining an Institution's Success from a Financial Standpoint

With respect to finances, I think there are only two directions: up or down. I do not believe in flat, since it is a non-viable direction. If you look at the pressures of managing a business school, you always need more, and you always need better. This all costs more money. With money, I can solve all of the other issues. Mine is definitely a commercial, private sector view of the educational marketplace.

The most important thing to recognize is that if you are at the upper end of the business school environment, there are no significant differences between public and private schools other than some of the constraints under which you operate. We have a procurement structure that is specified by the state, which is one definite constraint. Certain things such as undergraduate tuition are set much lower than the cost of providing education compared with private schools, which can recover their costs with tuition. So while there really are differences, the actual operations of both first-class public and private schools are technically the same. Thus, I do not think of public schools as our competition. Our competition is the best business schools in the country, regardless of their public or private status.

Determining the Popularity of an Institution

There are three major components that affect the public's perception of a school's reputation and popularity. The first is history. Part of what drives recognition of an institution is having been around a long time and having a strong alumni base. The second is marketing, which is dependent on how vividly and effectively the school's messages are communicated to the public. The third is producing world-caliber research in volume. The ability to do this generates academic respect, which then goes into generating public recognition.

External rankings are very important because people believe them. People make decisions based on numbers that may go up or down but are usually unrelated to the true quality of the institution. In the long term, it's the research position of the modern university that counts, and it takes time for that to be perceived.

As a result, there has to be a maniacal, dogmatic drive toward moving up in terms of quality. At the same time, you must build a marketing apparatus to tell people about it. I don't want to wait thirty years for people to figure out that in the year 2006 the Smith School was a great place.

I believe in communicating both positive and negative information honestly. For instance—and sometimes this backfires—if Smith is not rated as high as we should have been in a ranking I believe is methodically flawed, I will point that out. Some people think that is sour grapes, but I think that is essential because you can't accept someone else's image of what you are. It's like waking up Monday morning and discovering that the game you played on Sunday had a different score than the one you observed. You tell everyone as much as you can of the positive news.

Howard Frank was appointed dean of the Robert H. Smith School of Business in 1997. Under his leadership, the stature of the business school has advanced dramatically. Dr. Frank led the transformation of the school's curriculum and research agenda, integrating core business disciplines with such subjects as information technology, supply chain management, and e-commerce. Today, the Smith School is recognized as a world leader in management education and research for the digital economy.

Dr. Frank has served in both the public and private sectors and is widely recognized as a world-class information technology expert whose accomplishments include fundamental contributions to the development of the Internet. Prior to the Smith School, he served as director of the Defense Advanced Research Project Agency's Information Technology Office, where he managed a $300 million annual budget aimed at advancing the frontiers of information technology. He has been a member of the board of directors of more than a dozen telecommunications and computer companies and has experience in the venture capital and mergers and acquisitions fields, having led the acquisition or sale of a number of companies.

Dr. Frank is a prolific author, having written more than 190 articles and chapters in books on technology and the management of technology. He was an adjunct professor of decision sciences at the Wharton School and an associate professor of electrical engineering and computer sciences at the University of California at Berkeley. He received his M.S. and Ph.D. from Northwestern University and his B.S.E.E. from the University of Miami.

Nurturing the Enrichment Process

James C. Bean

Dean, Lundquist College of Business
University of Oregon

Acting as Dean of a Business School

People in traditional academic units tend to believe the deans of business schools only care about money rather than traditional scholarly ideals. To the contrary, I am from a background in liberal arts, and I spent twenty-four years in an engineering college before moving to business. I chose to come to Oregon because the faculty had such traditional, research-centered ideals.

Education is about the enrichment of lives; of students, literally changing the way they think critically and the knowledge they bring to any discussion or problem; of their abilities to interact socially with the network of people in their world; and of faculty and staff, who are creating new knowledge and sharing it with their students and the greater community. The college is really theirs. The role of the dean is to nurture this synergistic enrichment process by feeding it with the resources and intellectual climate necessary to breed excellence. We all have a tendency to regress to the mean. Keeping a pressure toward excellence is a critical responsibility of a dean.

The role of a dean at a business school does differ somewhat from the role of a dean at an undergraduate school. The primary difference in a business school environment is the closeness of ties with the business community. Science, engineering, and medicine have on-campus laboratories. Humanities and law have the libraries. Business relies on real operating companies as critical parts of its research and educational missions. A business dean needs exceptional relationships with the business community in addition to the relationships with students, faculty, staff, parents, boards, and administration.

In some aspects, being the dean of a school is a management position, just like any other industry. The main difference, in a word, is tenure. A dean in an academic institution is more like a rotating managing partner position rather than a chief executive officer. Tenured faculty members cooperate with the dean because they believe the direction of the college is positive and the dean can be trusted to further the quality of their organization. Maintaining trust and a sense of ownership among the faculty is critical to accomplishing anything.

Faculty and Staff

Deans work closely with the other academic deans, the various vice presidents, the provost and vice provosts, and the president. The key to working effectively with upper administration is shared vision. If the president, provost, other administrators, and other deans all share with you an understanding of the role of your unit in the university and its value to the collective of fields within the university, it is quite easy to collaborate and achieve your goals. Difficulties arise when key leaders have differing views of your college's role within the community. It is a never-ending communication task to maintain a shared vision.

The key players on our team within the college include the associate dean for academic affairs, the associate dean for professional affairs, the assistant dean for external affairs, the assistant dean for operations, and the assistant deans for undergraduate and graduate programs. The associate dean for academic affairs is responsible for academic quality control. He or she oversees hiring, promotion and tenure, curriculum development, space allocation, and faculty salaries. He or she is responsible for the academic link between the college and the university. The associate dean for professional affairs oversees the four signature centers, the Leadership Center, experiential education, and career services. He or she is responsible for the academic link between the college and the business community. The assistant dean for external affairs oversees development, alumni relations, and publications. He or she is responsible for fundraising and its attendant processes. The assistant dean for operations oversees finance and administration, facilities, and information technology. The assistant deans for undergraduate and graduate programs oversee recruiting students, reviewing applications, advising, and the care and feeding of matriculated students.

Each leadership position requires different skills. The associate dean for professional affairs should be a program builder. He or she will try to move the college to operate at the speed of business. The associate dean for academic affairs should be a traditionalist who seeks to ensure that we do not get too far beyond the comfort speed of the university and faculty. The assistant dean for external affairs is a development professional who also must be able to manage a significant staff and budget. This combination has proved challenging. The assistant dean for operations is a traditional management function requiring team-building skills, detail orientation, and expert knowledge of university policies and procedures. The program assistant deans must be excellent recruiters and marketers and must also nurture existing students. They deal with many knotty issues arising occasionally from students' personal crises, cheating, and less-than-satisfactory faculty/student interactions.

We have a very participative governance system. We come to good decisions on complex matters through active contribution by a variety of leaders in the college. I expect the team members to challenge proposals and provide alternatives. Once we come to an agreement, I expect team members to support it and explain to their constituencies why the collective came to that conclusion. As an example, last year we had salary raises for faculty. Due to state disinvestment in higher education following the events of September 11th, we had not had raises for about four years. We were essentially without process for allocating incremental funds to faculty, since the environment had changed so drastically during that period. A fundamental division within the faculty arose during initial discussion: should salaries be pegged to markets, which differ significantly between disciplines, or to performance? If the former, an average performer from a higher-paying discipline might be paid more than an outstanding performer from a lower-paying discipline. If the latter, we move away from market norms and risk losing faculty from higher-paying disciplines. Clearly, the answer is a combination of the two. But getting to the right combination was one of the most difficult discussions we have undertaken. We were successful because we gave the process time to anneal. A variety of solutions were put on the table, recombined, and massaged over several months. In the end, the compromise not only solved the immediate problem, but it provided a precedent for how to approach future raise opportunities and how we as an organization would engage difficult discussions.

Functioning Successfully as a Dean

The best piece of advice I ever received on leadership is to be honest and transparent. If the people grow to trust you, they will cut you slack when you need it. One piece of advice I find myself often giving to others comes from Thomas Paine: lead, follow, or get out of the way.

Long-term success is largely a function of trust built up with faculty, administration, and the business community. If they each believe you are listening to and being honest with them, they will forgive mistakes and decisions that do not go their way. When you recognize that you have made a mistake, admit it quickly and ask for help to get out of whatever mess you created. So long as it does not happen too often and the mistake is not too large, it can be a positive team-building experience. Anything you can do to build a sense of ownership among faculty and the business community is social capital in the bank. As an illustration, while our non-tenure track faculty members contribute greatly to our educational missions, they had been largely ignored in our policies and procedures. Many had not had performance reviews in some time. In an attempt to regularize the non-tenure track faculty, we developed a proposal for formalizing processes of hiring, promoting, and dismissing them. I presented it in a forum for non-tenure track faculty expecting accolades for finally recognizing their long-term value within the college. In reality, they saw it uniformly as an attack, and the hallway buzz grew ugly over the next two days while I was traveling. After speaking to a few members of the group to understand how they had perceived it, I issued an apology and explained what I had, unsuccessfully, been trying to achieve. We started over and a few months later held another forum to address the issues again. The group thanked me for apologizing, and the outcome was a much healthier relationship between the dean's office and the non-tenure track faculty as a group.

Too many people in any bureaucracy believe they best serve their organization by obstructing others' movements. The Paine quote often associated with Lee Iacocca best captures the path to success. I like to begin even difficult discussions with a straw person proposal. People find it easier to react and refine than to create solutions out of whole cloth. A proposal, even if a bad idea, can often lead another to a great idea. Our leadership team is well-accustomed to the fact that it cannot respond to one of the straw persons with the "get in the way response" of "I don't like it." Such a comment is received immediately with the question, "What is an alternative?" The acceptable response is to lead by providing a better answer, follow by signing on to the current solution, or don't participate.

The key to keeping your edge as the dean of a business school is to engage an administrative position with the same zeal and creativity you apply to your research activities. Then it never gets repetitive. If you feel that it is a service, different in creativity and fundamental engagement than what you would prefer to be doing, the daily grinds will become interminable.

I have developed some strategies I feel help me function successfully in my position. The first is to keep talking to people who know more than you do. It gives you a network of people keeping you up to date. The business world moves too fast for any one person to "do the reading."

Always deflect credit to others. If the organization is successful, the dean gets the credit, so you do not need credit for specific ideas. Naming all winning ideas for subordinates buys ownership in the decision. When a proposal becomes public, the more people who feel they are part owners of the idea, the more easily it will be accepted.

In the same way, always absorb blame yourself. If something goes wrong, even if it is entirely the fault of subordinates, you are responsible for putting it in their hands. Take the blame. It buys loyalty. People will be willing to take on harder and more politically dangerous tasks if they know you "have their backs."

It is critical to get continual feedback on all aspects of the college's programs. There are formal ways to get feedback—surveys, dean's undergraduate advisory committees, business advisory committees, faculty governance councils, and so on. The best information flow comes from staying out of your office. "Management by walking around" is as important in academia as it is in business. Faculty and students will stop in the hall to tip you off to some issue long before they will make an appointment to see you. A Toyota plant manager once told me it was not a good thing if his superior called his office and found him in. If he was doing his job, he was walking the plant floor. I try to live that to the extent the schedule allows. As an example, on one walk through the halls I came across a discussion between a faculty member and a student. The student was distressed because an analysis he had done for the investment club had been captured by a Web-crawler and discovered by a company that had not faired well in the analysis. The company had threatened legal action against the student even though the material was purely factual. The faculty member grabbed me as I walked by and asked what we might do. I chuckled at the invasion of a bit of reality into the ivory tower and referred the company's letter to the university general counsel. She quickly resolved the issue. On the up side, the analysis was also seen by a research firm overseas who contracted with the student to do more work like that for them. I suspect that more traditional channels would have resolved the issue the same way, but things moved much faster because I happened to be wandering by.

The biggest challenge in my position is balancing the needs and perspectives of the wide variety of stakeholders—faculty, students, university administration, business advisory boards—some of which have widely differing definitions of excellence. The best approach for meeting this challenge is a constant, compelling vision for where the college is going. The varying perspectives can be seen either as a set of warring factions competing for the heart of the college or as collaborators bringing their special strengths to build a future. The first step in getting to the latter description is to communicate a consistent, compelling vision before the various groups.

As mentioned above, one difficult issue we face is handling the relationship between tenure track and non-tenure track faculty in a research institution. The mantra within any research university is that our research enhances our education. The students are learning cutting-edge material. Yet in a business school, the non-tenure track faculty members are critical to a good program. How do we make sure they are not second-class citizens?

Our non-tenure track faculty is composed, typically, of former business professionals with a knack for teaching. They bring real experience to the classroom and experiential learning programs. They manage the time-consuming business contacts that are difficult for research faculty given their other duties. The non-tenure track faculty members bring important skills and experiences to the educational programs we neither expect nor breed in research faculty.

Every research institution in which I have served has had ongoing issues regarding the status of non-tenure track faculty. Here at Oregon, there were distinct issues with how the non-tenure track faculty were treated and perceived, and with their job satisfaction. To address the situation, we charged two committees. The climate committee consisted of leading non-tenure track faculty who surveyed their counterparts to develop a list of climate issues and to propose remedies. The academic committee consisted of tenure track and non-tenure track faculty, and it sought to remedy the concerns regarding hiring, review, promotion, and retention policies regarding non-tenure track faculty.

I met with the non-tenure track faculty in small groups and twice with the entire group to discuss issues and reports submitted by the committees. Some of these meetings were difficult and contentious, as noted earlier. Out of these discussions, some recommendations were implemented. We repaired the egregious misclassification of some individuals and named a non-tenure track ombudsperson. While progress has been made, this remains a potential problem area within the college and university. The university is currently finishing its own study on the matter that will provide some additional progress.

Other difficult situations regard personnel decisions. Hiring, tenure and promotion, and the awarding of named titles for faculty are the key filters to enriching the quality of the institution. Tenure denials and dismissing non-performing staff are very difficult but critically important processes. The key to handling these situations effectively is to separate someone's performance in this job from his or her value as a person. It is too often communicated to people being asked to leave an organization that "they just are not good enough." Someone in that position naturally rejects such a fundamental attack on his or her value as a human. The result is often grievances, lawsuits, or worse.

I find it much better to bolster the candidates' self-worth throughout, taking an approach of "this opportunity did not work out for the following reasons." Then I work with them to recognize where they were successful and how they can build that into successful opportunities elsewhere. Many leaders shy from the confrontational aspect of meeting with unsuccessful candidates. I believe it is more effective to meet frequently to hash over what happened, why it happened, and how they feel about it. While it is time-consuming, it is much more efficient than defending against lawsuits.

Changes for the Role of Dean: Past and Future

Challenges for people in my position also come from changes in the academic environment, how it interacts with the outside world, as well as reacting to changes in the world outside our doors. There have been massive changes in the environment of education over the past several years. For a decade, we have seen a demand for greater accountability from higher education, particularly for state schools. In the post-September 11th recession, state funding for public schools was cut dramatically. Few believe it will ever return to traditional levels. Yet many state legislatures have attempted to retain the level of control they exercised in the days of 40 to 50 percent state funding. Current state contribution to funding at Oregon is approximately 14 percent of the overall budget. While the legislature here is slowly freeing the universities to behave more as entrepreneurial entities, it is very much the case that leadership in a state university today is a political tightrope act, balancing accountability to the state, donors, parents, students, and faculty.

The education business has also changed dramatically due to the Internet and the opening of the Soviet bloc and China. Collaborations in Eastern Europe and East Asia provide access to huge education markets and exciting experiments in business growth, entrepreneurship, and organizational models.

The deans of the future will spend most of their time off campus, raising funds, and visiting distant partners. The traditional concept of the idyllic rural campus, where students and faculty retreat to think and create, is quickly succumbing to one of a home base in a highly connected network of universities and businesses across the world. The ranking leaders of the future will be those schools that develop the strongest global networks today.

Vision for the School

This change in academia reflects in competition among schools beyond the expected areas of athletics or academic recognition. The business school market is fiercely competitive, with something like 1,100 M.B.A. programs across the country. To be successful, we need to specialize, differentiate, and collaborate. Our faculty has chosen to build the college around four signature themes—sports business, innovation/entrepreneurship, securities analysis, and sustainable supply chain management. Each of these areas has strong footing in the Oregon economy and the strengths of our faculty. We will provide a unique education in each of these themes that will attract outstanding students from around the globe. We are a relatively small college, and to be successful at this goal, we must partner with other units within the university and state and around the world. We currently have joint programs with Oregon State University's colleges of arts and sciences, journalism and communications, and law. We also offer an executive M.B.A. in partnership with the business schools at Portland State and Oregon State. We are currently discussing new programs with Oregon's College of Architecture and Allied Arts, and Oregon State University's College of Engineering. Our relationships with Hanyang University in Korea, Fudan, and Shanghai Jiao Tong in China are critical to delivering on this promise.

Our college is committed to becoming world-renowned in a few niche areas, consistent with the mission of the University of Oregon and the culture and business climate of Oregon. The University of Oregon is a public, liberal arts, research university, and the Lundquist College is closely aligned with that mission. Our faculty and curricula have strong liberal arts associations.

To reach these goals, we must, of course, find ways to measure our success. We use multilayered success measures. In accordance with Association for the Advancement of Collegiate Schools of Business International policies, we are developing and implementing assurance of learning goals and metrics in all appropriate programs. Beyond that, we do exit surveys of students each year regarding their academic and social experiences in the college. We have also implemented a scorecard of numerical measures to track progress in key areas over time. We develop a set of objectives each year to represent the issues we plan to address in the coming year. In the first year of implementation, we graded ourselves at 75 percent success on reaching those objectives. Many sub-organizations develop finer grain objectives to contribute to the college-level objectives. The objectives were very useful in keeping the organization focused throughout the year.

Externally, people often use rankings as the measure of a college. Any educational institution is a combination of people (students, faculty, staff, administration), facilities (campus, labs, classrooms) and intellectual property (mission, curricula, policies and procedures, culture). Relative strengths vary from institution to institution. Even some of the greatest institutions in higher education are weak in one of these areas. Rankings attempt to combine all of those strengths and weaknesses into a single value. Rankings are important because prospective students, parents, and faculty read them. However, no administrator should manage to optimize the rankings. That allows someone else to set your objectives (such as a magazine editor). Each ranking defines a single objective function and compares all schools on that measure. The magazine's objective function will be relatively close to the real function for some schools and very far off for others. Luckily, the magazines all choose different functions. We are ranked sixty-third in graduate education and fifty-first in undergraduate by *U.S. News and World Report*, which has objective functions most closely aligned to large, comprehensive programs rather than specialty programs like ours. *Forbes* measures return on investment for a student, and we currently rank seventh among all programs with tuition under $40,000. *Princeton Review* ranks our facilities seventh among all business schools. *Sports Illustrated* has twice mentioned our sports business program as the premier program. Both *BusinessWeek* and *U.S. News and World Report* have ranked our innovation/entrepreneurship program sixteenth among approximately 800 such programs. My feeling is that you learn what you can from the rankings, develop your own goals and objectives appropriate to your school, and make the case publicly that you are making good progress on achieving those goals.

Capitalizing on Changes and External Feedback

Business sees changes approaching our schools many months before higher education does. By keeping in close contact with business advisory committees, we reap the benefits of their reconnaissance. Our challenge then is to react to this knowledge quickly, to the benefit of the school's growth and profit, but without becoming faddish or threatening core academic values.

I was attracted to Oregon partly because of the success of the university, college, business community, and philanthropic community coming together to build the magnificent Lillis Business Complex. The strategy for program growth in this college is to replicate this development achievement for the people and programs to inhabit the complex. We are roughly halfway to an $80 million campaign goal designed to take the college to a level of national and international recognition.

The business advisory councils also helped us develop a new strategy for executive education. The college has never engaged substantially in executive education, though a previous dean had founded a 501c3 to facilitate consulting and executive education. This past year, we began offering custom executive education programs. The start has been very successful, and we are looking to build infrastructure to expand our capacity. The drivers for executive education are threefold: it fulfills an important need for human resource development in the community; it drives faculty into closer contact with the business community, improving their teaching and research; and it provides additional resources for the college.

In order for the school to strike a balance between being a center for intellectual growth and a profitable institution, the college must have a shared vision of its mission. Most valid missions require both intellectual growth and financial resources. Many specific decisions trade off intellectual and financial alternatives. For example, should I hire an additional faculty member, or a director for executive education? The salary all comes from a single pot of money. The right decision can only be made looking at the current status of the college relative to its missions, goals, and objectives. We need to identify which option advances us closer to our goal. A successful institution is one that achieves its mission, goals, and objectives. Financial resources are one part of that quest.

Financial Implications and the Future

Just like any other successful business, expenses and income are important considerations in determining financial stability, growth, and success. Faculty salaries are substantially higher than in other fields. Due to a shortage of business faculty, top schools bid for faculty candidates like sports free agents. Fortunately, facilities are generally not as expensive for business schools as they are for more laboratory-oriented disciplines such as engineering, medicine, or sciences.

Tuition, of course, is a major factor in our revenue. In a state school, the fundamental tension is between access and the cost of education. The difference between the cost of education and what a typical citizen can pay was at one time borne by the people of the state through subsidy to the university system. Today, it is borne by private donors, parents, and the accumulation of debt by students. Ironically, the donors who provide the scholarships enabling many students to attend college today do so out of gratitude to the old state-funded system that gave them a start on a successful career. In many states, tuition is set too low to fund excellence, but high enough to prevent many citizens from attending.

In today's public school environment, state support only covers the basics. Private support makes the difference between basic and excellent. Decreased state funding affects our decision on what to charge our students for tuition. In Oregon, the sum of state allocation per student and tuition has descended over the past six years. While tuition has gone up a good deal, it has not kept pace with declining state support. Citizens claim tuition is rising quickly because of our inability to contain costs. In truth, it is transference of cost from the state government to the parents of students, with the university caught in the middle.

State disinvestment has driven many state schools, including Oregon, to behave more like private schools. Endowment has become an important determinant of excellence. Approaches to build a school's endowment vary greatly, given the legal environment of individual schools and states. In Oregon and many other states, endowments are managed by a private foundation. This foundation manages a fund of funds, where numerous money managers are allotted chunks of the endowment for investing. They are evaluated and reviewed, and the funds are moved to maintain an appropriate risk profile within the portfolio. The University of Oregon Foundation consistently realizes returns within the top 25 percent of university endowments.

Fundraising is an important aspect in helping to meet the goals of our school. The key to fundraising success is having a dream for what the school can become with private support, and communicating this dream effectively to potential donors. Those potential donors must be engaged in the activities of the college to develop a sense of ownership for the institution. When gifts are made, you must follow through and accomplish what was promised. It sounds simple, but it takes a great deal of time and effort.

We have just developed a new vision and mission statement for the college, and we are beginning to rebuild the college to achieve it. As we learn which components of the strategy are working and which do not meet the student market, faculty market, donor market, or employer market, we will adjust. The strategy is designed to allow that sort of flexibility. I look forward to the many interactions with faculty, students, and professionals, which will continue to guide us in an ever-improving direction. In my tenure, we will not perfect our vision of the Lundquist College. But the joy is in the process, the progress, and the lives that are enhanced through the journey.

James C. Bean is the Harry B. Miller professor and dean of the Lundquist College of Business at the University of Oregon. He was formerly a professor in the department of industrial and operations engineering at the University of Michigan. He has earned a master's degree and Ph.D. from Stanford University in operations research and a B.S. in mathematics from Harvey Mudd College. Professor Bean's research interests are in genetic algorithms, integer programming, and infinite horizon optimization as applied to equipment replacement, capacity expansion, asset management, production, and scheduling. He has published in Mathematics of Operations Research, Operations Research, Mathematical Programming, Management Science, IIE Transactions, Naval Research Logistics, The Engineering Economist, Interfaces, *the* Journal of Optimization Theory and Applications, INFOR, Engineering Design and Automation, Information Processing and Management, *and the* Journal of Biomechanics. *Professor Bean was associate dean for academic affairs and associate dean for graduate education for more than five years, and co-director of the Joel D. Tauber Manufacturing Institute for six years at the University of Michigan. He is an associate editor for the* Journal of Scheduling, *past associate editor of* Management Science, *and former editor of the* ORSA/TIMS Annual Comprehensive Index. *Professor Bean is past president of the Institute for Operations Research and the Management Sciences.*

Professor Bean has worked on various industrial projects with companies such as General Cable (production control), Penford Products (production scheduling), Homart Development (divestiture scheduling), General Motors (scheduling and equipment replacement/capacity planning), Michigan Consolidated Gas Company and IBM (equipment replacement), Bethlehem Steel (capacity planning), and Tektronix (forecasting). He was recently appointed by the governor as a technical advisor to the Oregon Innovation Council.

Dedication: *This chapter is dedicated to the faculty, staff, and students of the Lundquist College of Business at the University of Oregon.*

Maintaining the Momentum: The Experience of an Interim Dean

Rosa Oppenheim

Acting Dean

Rutgers Business School – Newark and

New Brunswick

The Role of Dean

Deans at a major business school within a large public research university are responsible for setting the strategic direction of the school. They establish priorities and make and implement decisions on all academic programs, including degree and executive education programs; domestic and international programs; faculty recruitment and development; student recruitment and retention; staff recruitment and development; outreach activities; and financial management. As such, deans and their staffs are involved with all of the school's constituencies: prospective students, current students, alumni, faculty, staff, campus and university administration, parents, the corporate community, funding agencies, and state legislators.

Business schools prepare students, at both the graduate and undergraduate levels, for meaningful and successful careers in management in both the for-profit and not-for-profit sectors. This is a more focused mission than that of an undergraduate arts and sciences school. At the same time, it requires much more contact with the external corporate and not-for-profit community for guidance, financial support, and internship and career opportunities for students.

At the Ph.D. level, however, the dean's role is closer to that of a graduate arts and sciences dean. Here, deans focus on training the next generation of researchers, which requires support for teaching and research assistants and for faculty seeking external grants to help support doctoral students.

Business School Vision

The fundamental purpose of a business school is to provide students at all levels with the skills necessary to successfully enter and progress in their management careers. As a New Jersey research-based business school with a global reach, we can best accomplish this by building a strong faculty possessing the ability to advance the theory, analysis, and practice of management; by developing a strategic focus in a limited number of areas in which we excel, including pharmaceutical management, supply chain management, financial management, and business ethics, and simultaneously offering a comprehensive business education at the undergraduate, master's, Ph.D., and executive education levels; by delivering a blend of theory and experiential knowledge to a diverse student body; and by creating meaningful connections to the business and not-for-profit community.

Our goals for the school are consistent with the mission of Rutgers University, which includes a commitment to research, teaching, and service. The primary goals for the school are to conduct internationally recognized research that advances the theory, methodology, teaching, and practice of management; to become a center for innovation and excellence in teaching where new ideas, concepts, and technologies invigorate up-to-date pedagogy; and to foster growth and development throughout the state and the region.

We endeavor to meet our research goal by allocating, where possible, resources for faculty research support; by the establishment and support of research centers in designated areas of excellence; by annual review of untenured faculty progress toward meeting explicit research goals and periodic post-tenure reviews; and by strategic hiring of tenure track and adjunct faculty to support excellence in our areas of specialization.

Attainment of our teaching goal requires regular monitoring of the teaching performance of each faculty member through the annual review with department chairs of the results of the university's student evaluation of each section taught; through regular review of course syllabi for relevance and thoroughness; and through departmental mentoring of junior faculty. In addition, we conduct ongoing assessment of student learning at all levels. To meet our goal of service to the community, we strive to advance the quality of life in the university, New Jersey, and beyond. At the community/state level, we use an extensive advisory board structure, as well as individual business leaders, to build meaningful linkages with business and non-profit organizations and to facilitate economic development and entrepreneurship through training, consulting, and special projects.

Our stated vision is to be a top-ranked, globally oriented business school providing excellent research and education, blending theory, practice, creativity, and critical thinking, and preparing our students to meet the challenges of a rapidly changing business environment. We seek to accomplish this vision through first-class research, strong linkages to the business community, high-quality learning involving a diverse body of students who have the desire to learn and grow through their education, and quality service to the citizens of New Jersey and beyond.

Dean Team

Most business school deans work closely with a cadre of high-level specialists. In my position, I work with a staff of associate deans, academic program directors, and directors of information technology, development, communications, and alumni. The associate dean for faculty and research manages the faculty recruitment, reappointment, tenure, and promotion processes, as well as seeks out and disseminates information on grant opportunities. The associate dean for academic programs manages all aspects of our degree programs, accreditation issues, and assessment of learning. The associate dean for administration is responsible for all personnel and budgetary functions, including assisting faculty in the preparation of grant proposals.

In addition, our team consists of department chairs who are responsible for faculty recruitment, development, and evaluation; setting a research agenda that is consistent with the strategic priorities of the school and university; curriculum development; and staffing of all courses. Other important positions include the directors of our admissions, student services, and career management offices, who interact directly with our students and ensure smooth and effective operation of these functions.

Management of faculty and staff in education differs from management in other industries in terms of the ultimate goals of the organization. There is, relatively speaking, less focus on the bottom line or responsibilities to shareholders. The stakeholders in education form a much broader base, including employees, students, parents, alumni, corporate partners, and for a public university like ours, the citizens of the state.

A significant difference between managing in education versus managing in other industries is the existence of the tenure system in education. While this offers necessary protections for faculty, it also means management cannot resort to "brute force"—it must motivate and influence people using carrots rather than sticks.

As a result, business school deans typically look for colleagues who display intelligence; creative and proactive thinking and behavior; diligence; integrity; attention to detail; dedication; good communications skills; the ability to get along with others; empathy with others, especially students; and perhaps most important, a good sense of humor.

Measuring Success

Most business school deans measure success in a combination of lofty and mundane ways. One of the most important benchmarks is the quality of faculty research, as measured by the academic journals in which it appears. The quality of placement of our Ph.D. students is another important measure; most business schools aspire to place graduates in educational institutions whose quality is at least comparable to their own. At the M.B.A. level, business school deans measure success by the quality of incoming students, as measured by diversity, professional experience, undergraduate grade point average, and GMAT scores, and by their success in securing productive internships and permanent career positions at graduation and throughout their careers. At the undergraduate level, most business schools measure success by incoming quality, diversity, retention, internships, and career placement. At all levels, deans assess student learning and student satisfaction. And most, alas, cannot afford to ignore the national rankings, despite their flaws.

To achieve these goals, most business school deans use long-term strategies. As an acting dean serving the school during a period of great uncertainty in terms of leadership and budgets, my strategies for helping the school grow are more for the short term than they would be for a permanent dean. I try to identify and promote initiatives that engage the faculty and enable the school to continue to improve and respond to the needs of our constituencies. These initiatives include, for example, a focus this academic year on curriculum reform at the undergraduate and M.B.A. level; expansion of revenue-producing endeavors such as international programs; incentives for faculty for grant writing; and involvement of faculty and staff in plans for relocation to a new facility.

Challenges to Success

As an under-funded public institution, one of our biggest challenges is to be competitive in the market for new faculty in terms of salary, course loads and scheduling, and research support. We allocate discretionary revenue, obtained from off-site and international programs and from tuition surcharges, toward enhancing faculty salaries and summer support, and offering research grants on a competitive basis. Successful fundraising is an ongoing challenge: many business disciplines have relatively few sources for outside grants, and our ability to grow as a faculty and as a school depends on our relationships with the corporate community and our ability to attract funding in support of research and academic programs. Fundraising is critical to a dean's long-term success.

Deans face a variety of challenges in their positions. In my job, I have found that balancing our needs with a critical budget situation in our state is the most difficult situation I have faced. It has required tough decisions with respect to cutting departmental budgets, staff layoffs, and limited faculty recruitment. We have tried to maintain hiring in our strategic areas of excellence and seek additional sources of revenue at the same time that we cut costs.

Personnel situations periodically require sensitive handling, particularly when they involve tenured faculty. These are best approached by using the power to persuade rather than compel. I have also found that faculty members often assume the dean's office has both unlimited resources and unlimited power to make things happen. We have often thought that if every faculty member could be "dean for a day," there would be a clearer understanding of the constraints under which the administration operates.

Keeping an Edge

At a business school, as at many institutions, people are the most valuable resource. At our school, we have been fortunate in having a team of associate deans, program directors, and chairs who are deeply committed to the school and university. Despite differences in philosophy, everyone's goal is to achieve and maintain excellence in research, teaching, and service.

Treating people with respect is the most effective strategy for success in any position, especially in a university setting. By articulating a shared vision and the will to work together to make it happen, cooperation is encouraged and goals can be met. An open door policy and willingness to listen encourages people to communicate their problems and ideas for moving the school ahead.

Most deans receive ongoing feedback from all constituencies. At our school, we conduct university-wide student evaluations of all sections of all courses every semester, and we share the results with students, faculty, chairs, and administration. We also incorporate these results into decisions on reappointment, tenure, and promotion. Student satisfaction surveys, exit surveys of graduating students, alumni surveys, and regular evaluations of untenured faculty (annually) and tenured faculty (every five years) ensure a continuing stream of information in all directions. Our associate dean for academic programs is responsible for assessment at all levels, which is accomplished through a formal procedure for gathering, sharing, and acting on this information.

Management Style

Every dean has a distinct management style. Mine can be summarized as "Be nice. Be fair. Work hard." I believe in the golden rule: do unto others as you would have them do unto you. And I try to remember that no one in an organization, especially me, is indispensable.

This reminds me of the departing business school dean who visits his replacement during her first week in the new position. He hands her three numbered envelopes, with the advice that whenever she encounters a crisis, she open one of the envelopes. Several months later, she opens envelope number one and finds a piece of paper with the words, "Blame your predecessor." She does so, and the brewing calamity is averted. Sometime later, she realizes it is time for envelope number two, and she finds the words, "Appoint a faculty committee." Once again, disaster is avoided. At signs of the next catastrophe, she opens envelope number three and reads, "Prepare three envelopes."

Changes Coming

A business school dean today must be particularly sensitive to the rapid economic, political, technological, and social changes that occur, all of which affect curriculum, faculty and student recruitment, budgeting, fundraising, and other areas. These changes have had a major effect on the nature of the education industry in general and certainly on business education. To prepare students for the careers they will be entering upon graduation, business schools must train them to be effective decision-makers in the face of a changing environment and to set priorities that can respond to such an environment.

Probably the change with the greatest long-term effect is the incorporation of technology into business school education. It not only affects the educational process itself, but it also alters students' preparation for lifelong careers and learning. The education industry must be flexible to adapt to such changes.

I also anticipate that it will become increasingly important to attract a portfolio of talents to our faculty mix. While research accomplishments remain a primary goal for all tenured and tenure track faculty, as a full-service business school on multiple campuses, we must attract experienced practitioners to the classroom as well. We do this by hiring limited term instructors, whose responsibilities are more heavily weighted toward teaching; by hiring clinical professors, who bring valuable and specific business experience to our students; by engaging executives-in-residence who present guest lectures and work with faculty and administration to share their management expertise; and, in our specialty programs such as pharmaceutical management, by bringing industry experts in to team-teach courses and mentor students.

Creating Balance

All business schools must balance maintaining intellectual growth with increasing costs. Faculty salaries and support are the biggest expenses we have. At our school, we embark on revenue-enhancing initiatives that are consistent with our goals as a research institution. Thus, in expanding our international programs in China, we have established an Asian Research

Center that encourages faculty to combine their teaching experiences in Asia with their research agendas, for the mutual benefit of both. We also allocate funds from revenue-producing activities and fundraising to the support of research, especially for new faculty, in terms of summer support and competitive research grants and stipends. Our use of a portfolio of faculty enables us to maintain a lower teaching load for research-active faculty at the same time that we hire instructors who can offer valuable business expertise to our students.

Our efforts at revenue generation are consistent with our mission as a state university. Hence, we offer off-site M.B.A. courses at multiple corporate locations throughout the state, in an attempt to bring education to the workplace and nearer to home. Similarly, our international executive M.B.A. programs in China foster research opportunities for faculty, as well as generate revenue for the school. Tuition surcharges for business students and summer school revenues enable us to provide summer support to new faculty, offer funds for travel to conferences for Ph.D. students, and enhance travel funding and research support for faculty.

Tuition

As a state institution, tuition covers a relatively small portion of our costs; annual tuition increases are limited by the state legislature. Tuition revenues are collected by the central administration. Only recently has the university moved to all-funds budgeting, where we actually receive a fixed percentage of the tuition generated by our programs. We have implemented a tuition surcharge or program fee in several programs (undergraduate, executive M.B.A.) that provide additional funds for the school. Decreasing state budgets and increasing costs have led to annual tuition increases, but the amount is limited by the state legislature.

Our long-term goals for our funding are to establish an increased number of named chairs in order to attract faculty of a caliber that will bring us to the next level in terms of research achievements and national recognition; to occupy a state-of-the-art facility that will, like our Global Markets Financial Center, enhance the student experience and promote faculty research; to provide adequate scholarship support to attract a top-quality and diverse student body; and to build upon existing strengths such as pharmaceutical management, supply chain management, business ethics, financial management, and management of technology.

The school sets its fundraising goals by working closely with the development staff, the university foundation, and the board of advisors in setting goals and priorities, identifying potential donors, and articulating our vision.

We know we have been successful when we have been able to reward faculty appropriately for their contributions to the school's growth and reputation; recruit top people, at both junior and senior levels, in the disciplines of strategic importance to the school; provide the necessary resources and support services for faculty research, grantsmanship, innovative teaching and learning, and a positive and constructive student experience; maintain state-of-the-art, safe, comfortable, and adaptable facilities; and provide the amenities necessary for an environment conducive to learning for students, faculty, and staff.

Institutional Popularity

Prospective students learn about a business school through word-of-mouth endorsements from current students and recent alumni; accomplishments of prominent alumni in their own organizations and industries; public and press recognition in the form of national rankings and other publicity about particular programs, faculty research, outreach achievements, and students; an informative, attractive, and easy-to-navigate Web site; advertising and promotional materials; and the reputation of the school and its faculty among other institutions.

Most business schools—ours included—see national rankings as flawed reflections of what a particular school has to offer to a particular student. Nevertheless, external rankings have a very significant affect on the size, quality, and diversity of the applicant pool, and hence on the quality of incoming students. Improving national rankings results in better student job placements, more prominent alumni, more successful fundraising, increased resources to support faculty recruitment and research, and measurable improvements in the quality of the school and its programs. As a result, it is difficult to discount their importance.

However, many schools—ours included—prefer to emphasize their particular programs that take advantage of the school's geographical location and corporate strengths. For instance, we have established a Pharmaceutical Management Research Center through a significant gift from Irwin and Blanche Lerner, and a corresponding M.B.A. concentration to respond to the needs of "the nation's medicine chest" in New Jersey, and a Supply Chain Management Center and corresponding M.B.A. concentration to respond to port security issues in the region. We have also created other niche activities that support the community, such as our Business and the Arts Program, which has established a GlassRoots program to train disadvantaged youth in glass-blowing and entrepreneurship. While national rankings are important, they often fail to draw attention to our involvement in the issues of the surrounding community and region, such as our Small Business Development Corporation and work with minority-owned businesses.

Positioning the School

Properly positioning a business school within the public eye requires a strong and effective business communications department with access to the local and national press and the resources to support an informative, attractive, and up-to-date Web site. Business leaders, university officials, and prospective students constantly remind the school of the need to publicize its strengths.

Probably the most important reason to focus on the positioning of the school is to enable it to attract a talented and diverse faculty willing to learn new methodologies, adopt new technologies for research and teaching, and adapt to change in the marketplace and in academia. We have found that an entrepreneurial spirit among the administration and faculty enables us to target new initiatives (such as programs and research centers) that respond to changes both within and outside the university. Thus, at the same time that we focus on a limited number of areas of strategic importance, we must be open to emerging trends and opportunities.

The Impact of Technology

Technology has changed the nature of learning in fundamental ways. The integration of technology into the curriculum has made business education more relevant to the needs of the business world. At our school, our early and rapid adoption of wireless technology enabled our faculty and students to respond to educational needs in management quickly and to train students in the traditional disciplines in a more useful and efficient way. Our move to Blackboard, a user-friendly course management system, was adopted by nearly our entire faculty within about a year, enabling enhanced faculty/student and student/student communication, course coordination, and assessment of learning.

Our experience with online learning has been mixed. Increased one-to-one communication between students and faculty requires smaller classes than we have had, and student reactions to courses taught exclusively online have been varied. Our faculty has been reluctant to embrace online courses without significant support for course development, generally in terms of course release time. We have had some limited success with a hybrid model—a combination of online sessions and periodic in-person sessions. As a multi-campus business school, our experience with distance learning technology has been most effective in minimizing faculty travel between campuses: departmental meetings, faculty seminars, and administrative meetings are regularly conducted by video-conferencing.

Keeping the School on Track

To be sure our activities continue to support our strategic goals, we engage in a periodic review of our strategic plan, involving a high-level faculty planning committee that is advisory to the dean, consultation with the dean's cabinet, and significant input from our faculty and board of advisors. This review typically occurs every five years, with changes considered on an ongoing basis. Our expectation is that when a permanent dean is appointed, the dean will initiate a new strategic planning process that will incorporate his or her vision into our plans for the future.

Rosa Oppenheim is currently acting dean and a professor of management science and information systems at Rutgers Business School in Newark and New Brunswick. She joined the school in 1973. Previously, she has served as associate dean for faculty and research (2002 to 2006), associate dean for academic programs (1993 to 2002), and director of the Teaching Excellence Center at Rutgers-Newark (1992 to 1993). She served as acting dean at Rutgers Business School in 1998.

Ms. Oppenheim is a co-author of Quality Management *(McGraw-Hill), now in its third edition, and of* Stat City: Understanding Statistics through Realistic Applications *(Richard D. Irwin), and has authored journal articles on total quality management, time series analysis and forecasting, the mathematical analysis of literary style, and integer programming. She has provided executive training for many corporations and has won numerous teaching awards.*

Dedication: *To Alan Oppenheim.*

Be Open, Be Honest, and Don't Take Yourself Too Seriously

Bill N. Schwartz

Dean, Silberman College of Business

Fairleigh Dickinson University

The Business School Dean's Role

I view my primary function as dean as that of facilitator. In my role, it is critical that I establish an image of someone who has integrity, enthusiasm, and the strong desire to move the institution forward both on an individual and a professional level. Certainly, the dean has responsibilities to all constituents including students, faculty, alumni, and parents, and these obligations vary depending on the issue and audience at hand. Overall, the dean's primary responsibility is to approach the job with honesty, openness, a willingness to listen, and above all, an unwavering commitment to doing all he or she can to fulfill the needs of each constituency.

The role of a dean at a business school does differ from the role of a dean at an undergraduate school, as well as from the roles of deans at law and medical schools. However, much like the roles of deans at law and medical schools, a business school dean's role includes a critical constituency that does not usually affect undergraduate deans: the current or future employers of the students. Students enroll in a vocational-based unit because they seek employment or improved status in a particular field. The dean of a business school must recognize the importance of that constituency and try to incorporate their presence in the unit in as many ways as possible. Some ways he or she can do this is to invite them to be members of advisory boards, guest lecturers, adjunct instructors, and providers of student and faculty internships, just to name a few inclusive roles. The dean must ensure that the educational process blends the ideas of both faculty and the business community to provide students with relevant subject matter. In this way, the roles of deans at business, medical, and law schools differ from undergraduate deans, who are not as heavily focused on external constituencies and potential employers.

The Purpose of a Business School

Ideally, a business school should operate in a collegial environment, with administrators functioning with faculty members in a cooperative and supportive environment. The attitude and spirit should be one of shared governance, mutual respect, and active debate on important and relevant issues affecting the school's mission and goals. The fundamental purpose of the school is to provide a relevant and challenging learning experience for students who actively engage in learning with the goal of applying the knowledge and skills they gain to interesting and rewarding business environments. Student learning should be facilitated by dedicated faculty members using a variety of pedagogical techniques while sharing and disseminating knowledge they have assimilated or generated.

The Silberman College of Business is a bi-campus unit and one of four colleges at the university. Becton College at our Florham Campus offers liberal arts and sciences instruction at the undergraduate level primarily. University College at our Metropolitan Campus offers liberal arts and sciences, as well as a host of professional programs at the master's and doctoral levels. Petrocelli College offers continuing education and a large number of varied programs both on and off campus.

Goals for Business Schools: Establishing and Executing the Vision

I have multiple goals for the business school itself. First, we must psychologically embrace the thrust of Association for the Advancement of Collegiate Schools of Business International (AACSB) accreditation, which is to strive for continuous improvement and thorough assessment. Second, we must serve the multiple constituencies we service by providing innovative and relevant academic programs, particularly at the graduate level. Our university wishes to be the leader in global education, which correlates with the academic programs we have and are planning in order to bring the world to our students and send our students to the world.

We need to evaluate, observe, and assess our activities consistently to determine the extent to which we are making progress toward accomplishing our mission. Hard work, commitment, and unwavering focus are critical components in achieving our goals.

The vision for our school depends upon a strong leadership plan. "Leadership" is a complex term and has many facets. We lead by word and by deed, with ideas and with actions. Ideas and proposals can stimulate others, and the process of working on the ideas and proposals provides examples that those we lead may emulate. Further, personal contact and positive mental attitude can attract adherents of our vision who can support our efforts.

In addition to sufficient funding, business schools need to focus on reasonable and rational goals and imbed them within the AACSB philosophy of continuous improvement to stimulate actions and avoid complacency. Even the highest-rated schools continually reexamine whether they can improve the programs they offer.

When measuring the success of our school and determining the effectiveness of our goals and strategy, AACSB accreditation maintenance is a primary external measurement. We also use standard direct and indirect assessment techniques. Most important is a faculty performance evaluation system, including a planning apparatus that stimulates faculty members to be the best they can be. We want to inspire our faculty members to strive to be consistently better while also feeling happy and positive about how they are doing.

Working Within the Organization: the Dean's Team

As business school dean, I report directly to three provosts: the university provost, who is in charge of academic affairs, and two campus provosts, who are in charge of a multitude of non-academic responsibilities. In order to work effectively with and for them, I need to understand their responsibilities and have empathy for their time commitments, both at work and outside of school. Cooperation and success come most easily from openness, mutual respect, honesty, and trust.

The key players of my team include an associate dean, five department chairs, three academic directors, and three administrative directors. The associate dean has a wide range of responsibilities internal to the college and the university. With respect to the department chairs, each one chairs a department of ten to fifteen people with at least two academic disciplines in each department. Then a pair comprised of an academic director and administrative director work with executive programs, another pair works on graduate and global programs, and the third pair handles undergraduate programs.

When putting together this team, there are certain skills that are critical for individuals to possess, given the demanding nature of academia and the unique nature of this environment. As such, I looked for team members who are creative and unafraid to present ideas. I also seek employees who have demonstrated a strong ability to work well as part of a team and a willingness to express their feelings, particularly if they do not agree with the prevailing direction of a discussion.

The Education Field Versus Other Industries

The major difference between managing in the field of education and managing in any other field can be summed up in one word: tenure. Job assurance and, in many cases, salary increases that are not based on merit result in a significant difference in the managerial process. Performance evaluation and minimal assessment make academia a very challenging environment because the system relies almost totally on pride of work to stimulate productivity.

In addition to the managerial challenges posed by tenure, the dean faces many other obstacles as well. Working with tight budgets that do not allow us, by anyone's fair observation, to do many of the things that must be accomplished to provide the students with the best and most stimulating learning experience represents one major challenge. A second major challenge is inspiring faculty members to maintain their vitality and excitement with their work after they are granted tenure and move toward the later stages of their careers.

A dean also faces many difficult situations in this position. One common situation is the need to terminate an individual prior to a tenure decision. The knowledge that this is the proper thing to do does not make the execution of this decision any easier. To overcome this challenge, I explain the situation to the individual and offer to help find a place with a better fit for him or her. We do not pull any punches, but we do try to be as compassionate as possible.

Another challenging situation is taking an open faculty position from one department and giving it to another. We try to establish a set of criteria and ask every department to provide the necessary information. Collectively, our executive team, including all the chairs, examines the data and tries to come to an understanding as to what we should do with respect to this position. Certainly turf battles occur, but these are lessened when I am not in a position of making a "data-free decision" unilaterally.

There is no major formula to overcoming these challenges, but I have found that remaining positive, listening to how other deans approach their duties, being supportive, and continually trying new approaches are effective skills and habits for overcoming these obstacles. In the face of these challenges, there are certain attributes a dean must possess in order to achieve long-term success on behalf of his or her school. These attributes include a positive attitude, a concern for students, personal pride, openness to change, and a good atmosphere in which to work that includes supportive colleagues and a cooperative central administration.

Biggest Misconceptions about the Role of a Business School Dean

The biggest misconception is the notion that the dean has a great deal of power. Specifically, this misconception relates to the amount of money we control. Frequently, we have less than 25 percent of our budget available as discretionary, and much of that covers operating expenses that really provide minimal discretion. Private endowment funds often have stipulations that limit access. In contrast, many people, both within the institution and externally, tend to assume we have a much larger budget than we do and fewer restrictions placed on the use of that money.

Helping the School Grow and Achieve Greater Profit

My philosophy with respect to being a strong and respected leader centers upon being open, straightforward, focused, and true to who I am. Most deans do not stay long in a position; the usual span in this role is about three to four years. I want to be able to look in a mirror and say I did the best I could do and feel good about myself. If I follow the philosophy I have just described, I can do that.

With respect to helping the school grow and achieve greater profit, I establish a marketing committee and a marketing plan. I ensure that the committee is composed of marketing faculty members and individuals with practical, real-world marketing experience.

A second tactic is to provide incentives for individuals to develop specialized programs toward niches we have not served. For example, we try to identify special groups of people or professional organizations that might be interested in a program developed specifically for their needs. Frequently, these programs have returned high gross margins and thus help our overall financial picture. The programs can offer additional teaching, travel, or consulting opportunities to the individuals who develop and participate in the program.

The Importance of Feedback

It is critical to the success of our institution that we receive and respond to honest and reliable feedback. Such feedback provides indirect assessment of the college's mission, objectives, plans, and programs, and we collect it through surveys of students, alumni, employers, and other members of the business community. In terms of faculty feedback, I select a limited number of faculty members whose opinions I value and trust. I often seek this feedback prior to making decisions so I can use their input to guide my decision-making process. I also use my dean's advisory committee to formulate plans and solutions based on our in-depth discussion of issues.

It is also important to keep one's edge as the dean of a business school by staying on top of emerging information, both within one's school and externally. I have found that a variety of tasks and the opportunities to work with interesting people both inside and outside the university help me keep my edge. I have breakfasts or lunches with members of the business community from our board of advisors as well as others, and I attend the meetings of the Chamber of Commerce and other professional associations (i.e., the CPA Society, the National Association of Corporate Directors). I have encountered many informative and interesting people. The most important resources are my colleagues and the wonderful alumni and members of the business community with whom I work on a frequent basis.

Throughout the years, I have received solid advice with respect to heading an institution. The best advice I have received with respect to decision-making is to listen, seek input, and then, once the decision is made, be comfortable with what I have decided. Other advice that has served me well is to distinguish between "little wars" and "big wars" when determining whether to get involved with certain issues. I have tried to pass on advice that was given to me and, more importantly, offer assistance to others as a person willing to listen. By following the philosophy I have outlined above, I hope to provide advice by example as well.

Recent Changes to the Role of a Dean

The dean's role always has been and should continue to be the role of manager. The issues the dean manages may change, but the job itself should not. Recently, the education industry has changed, as there has been less money available to both private and public institutions. We have also faced quantum changes in the use of technology, particularly in distance learning.

Distance learning poses another interesting challenge—to decide whether and/or to what extent we embrace it. We have to ask ourselves, how does this method of instructional delivery fit into our mission? If it does, in what ways will we use it (i.e., what mode(s) will we consider)? How do we train faculty to do it effectively?

Another recent change that has affected my role is that we face an aging professoriate with a different academic perspective from their younger colleagues. In addition, the gulf between the student perspective on what constitutes learning and the perspective of the faculty continues to become more pronounced. Students and faculty are from very different generations. Learning and life experiences are quite different and pose substantive difficulties for meaningful communication.

In terms of the business school specifically, employers have been providing less financial support for degree programs for their employees. A recent trend is that employers are doing more of their "education" in-house.

In the coming years, continuing progress in technology and greater emphasis on a global society will require anyone who fills the role of dean to gain considerable skills in the areas of technology and corporate culture to be successful and to lead a business school.

The Three Golden Rules for a Business School Dean

Every dean faces a different set of challenges depending on his or her school, faculty, location, and specific skill set. However, there are some basic rules that will serve any dean well, regardless of his or her circumstances.

1. *Be open.* Anything you have to hide, you should never do in the first place.

2. *Be honest.* There will always be someone smarter than you, so there is no point trying to outsmart everybody. Tell the truth; no matter what happens, you will be able to look at yourself in the mirror.

3. *Do not take the job too seriously.* No dean has ever received a Nobel Prize. We do a lot of good things, but life will go on with or without you in your position.

Being a Center for Intellectual Growth and a Profitable Institution: Striking a Balance

If a school encourages faculty to conduct research relevant to current issues facing the school's constituencies, the work produced can help people in the community and those in the classrooms. Students can take what they have learned and, enriched by the relevant research the faculty has conducted, apply it to their work environment. By doing that consistently, the institution will be profitable through word of mouth and will help its constituencies profit from what the school is doing, both inside and outside of the classroom.

A business school offers unique ways to make money. Specialized programs developed for niches can make significant money if the business school can work arrangements with a central administration to split the profits. Centers and institutes can be very profitable if they are allowed to be entrepreneurial and to reap some benefit from their activities.

The most expensive element of operating a business school is not related to technology or facilities; rather, an overwhelming 85 percent of our budget is allocated to salary and salary-related items.

Determining Tuition

When determining tuition, we are more cost-driven than market-analytic. We do use analytical models that project future enrollments, but they are based on past enrollments for the most part. Like most schools, we have difficulty quantifying the revenue side but have fairly controllable cost structures. One of our major enrollment sources is international students. Certainly, visa access and political unrest can affect us. Our other enrollment source is regional domestic students. Local and regional economic trends can affect us as well.

From a financial standpoint, I believe a school is successful if it is able to finance important programs and build the facilities necessary to provide the best quality education for the students.

Building the School's Endowment

A school's endowments are derived partly from aggressive cultivation, partly from alumni activities, and frankly, partly from luck. In the long run, treating students well and being sure they leave happy, which in the case of a business school means with a good job, are the most important methods of endowment development. It is important to remember when working with current students that you are also dealing with future alumni.

With respect to the investment of our endowments, we invest our funds within the university's portfolio. We do not have independent access and activities.

In terms of fundraising, our college is just beginning to do fundraising on its own. Previously, everything was centralized. We are currently at the stage of "friend-raising" and cultivating relationships.

The trustees also have an important role with respect to the finances of our institution. The trustees set financial policy. We have a very active and involved group who meet frequently.

Factors that Drive an Institution's Popularity

Word of mouth is the strongest factor driving our recognition popularity. We must keep our students happy.

External rankings are extremely important to all schools but particularly to the most elite. For us, word of mouth and relationships with high school advisors and counselors in the region is critical to our success.

Positioning Your School to Thrive on Change

As we face emerging trends and dynamic changes in the marketplace, it is essential to stay in close touch with external constituencies in order to seek advice and counsel about what is going on with their businesses. Armed with this information, we are able to determine what we can do to incorporate those things into our curriculum. This is simply what the AACSB calls "continuous improvement."

With respect to technology and online learning, these components have had—and will continue to have—a powerful impact on the way traditional schools operate. Information technology and distance learning have made the global marketplace smaller and have added significantly to the competition each institution faces, particularly at the graduate level. It also forces schools to consider carefully what they can and should do, as well as what they cannot and should not attempt. If schools spread themselves too widely, they risk not being attentive to their core programs and constituencies, and not devoting sufficient resources to that which has been successful in the past.

In planning our strategy for the future, it is essential that we review our strategic and tactical plans annually and consider significant changes at least every three years. It is a dynamic and fluid process, so we can adapt in a way that addresses external and unexpected changes.

Bill N. Schwartz Ph.D. (UCLA) and CPA is dean of the Silberman College of Business at Fairleigh Dickinson University. Previously, he was dean of the School of Business and Economics at Indiana University at South Bend. He also served on the faculties at Virginia Commonwealth University, Temple University, and Arizona State University. He currently is co-editor of Advances in Accounting Education, *was editor of* Research on Accounting Ethics, *and was co-editor of* Advances in Accounting. *He has published more than fifty articles in academic and professional journals and has made fifty presentations of papers at academic meetings. He is a past chair of the teaching and curriculum section of the American Accounting Association and was named Virginia Accounting Educator of the Year in 1996.*

The Exciting and Challenging Business School Environment

Robert D. Reid

Dean, College of Business

James Madison University

The Role of a Business School Dean

A dean's primary role is that of a leader. He or she sets the direction for the school, establishes and supports the culture, and leads the efforts of others to achieve these stated goals and objectives. A business dean's role can be divided into several major areas. Within the college, the dean's primary responsibility is to provide leadership for defining a mission and vision, developing a strategic plan, securing resources, implementing plans, assessing performance against objectives, and ensuring continuous improvement.

Beyond this broad and important role, a dean has responsibility for the following functional areas: academic affairs, student services, external relations and development, and human resources and operations. Depending on the size, structure, and complexity of the business school, each of these functions may be staffed by an associate/assistant dean or director, as well as additional faculty and staff members.

In addition to the intra-business school focus, a dean is likely to be involved in other university-based functions such as working collaboratively with the university president, provost, and other deans and campus leaders on specific projects. These projects might cut across divisions or areas of the university and may involve the board of visitors or university trustees. Examples of such projects include campus-wide curriculum development, development or fundraising, and strategic planning for the university.

The Fundamental Purpose of a Business School

A business school has three fundamental purposes: teaching, scholarship, and service. The mission and supporting vision statements should establish and guide the way the business school attempts to compete in the educational marketplace. They should also define and promote a competitive uniqueness or brand for the school. What is the distinctive competency of the school? What is the school most known for?

Teaching is the most visible of the school's three purposes. Depending on the nature of the student body, the focus might range from a solely undergraduate emphasis to one that includes master's- and/or Ph.D.-level degree programs. The specific focus will be determined by the school's mission and relative emphasis on each level of academic program or degree. Business schools play an important role in educating the next generation of business leaders, and this is a role that should not be taken lightly.

The fundamental purpose of scholarship is less visible. The faculty, individually and collectively, should work to advance theory and knowledge. They should develop new knowledge and test theories in the work of application and practice. Each faculty member should have a personal research agenda that supports the research priorities of his or her department and college. Each individual's research agenda should focus on one—or two at most—of the following areas: discipline-based research, educational practice or pedagogy, or contributions to professional practice. The portfolio of research conducted by the faculty members of a particular school should be developed based on the mission of the school. For example, if a school has a large Ph.D. program, the research focus should be placed on discipline research. If a school has only an undergraduate student body, a higher emphasis on education and pedagogy research may be more appropriate.

Finally, each business school fulfills a service component. A portion of the faculty and staff's service efforts are focused internally on ways that help the school and university function more effectively. Secondly, faculty members provide service to their discipline and areas of expertise. For example, a faculty member might serve as a board member or officer of a professional association related to his or her discipline, or the faculty member might serve on the editorial board of a professional journal in his or her field of expertise. The range of professional contributions is quite broad, and the entire faculty of a business school will typically have a wide portfolio of service engagements. Finally, a business school provides services to the community. For example, the business school might be involved in economic development activities such as attracting new businesses to the area or providing executive education.

Building a Successful and Collaborative Team

First and foremost, when looking for a new member of our team, I seek someone who is a self-motivated person and has demonstrated leadership skills in his or her prior professional experience. A second desirable quality is the ability to develop a vision and help others conceptualize visions and make them reality. It is critical that the person have the ability to link mission, vision, and action plans. Failure to implement plans successfully results in failing to achieve potential and often leads to frustration among those who developed the vision and plan. A third skill is the ability to facilitate within a group. Any successful academic leader must be able to work effectively with a broad range of individuals, often within the same department. Strong facilitation skills are therefore important. A major component of being a good facilitator is being a good listener and being the type of individual who can draw the best ideas from the team members, creating something that is better than any one individual might have created.

On a broader scale, I have found it very useful to employ Steven Covey's *The 7 Habits of Highly Effective People* as a benchmark for effective leaders in an academic setting. The skills or habits discussed in this book include:

- *Being proactive.* With this habit, one does not simply react to a situation, but instead asks, "How can I anticipate what will happen and be ready to respond in a positive manner?"
- *Beginning with the end in mind.* To do this, ask, "Where are we going? What do we want to accomplish? How will we know when we achieve it? What does each of us have to accomplish if we are to achieve our goals?"
- *Putting first things first.* It is important to ask yourself if you can keep your focus on the important goals and objectives.
- *Thinking in a win-win way.* Determine how you can work with others so everyone can "win" and not feel as though they have lost out. What is important for others to attain? How can you help them attain what they are seeking and achieve what you or the team wants to accomplish as well?
- *Seeking first to understand, then to be understood.* Listen and fully understand the other person's position before you begin to state your own ideas or position.

- *Synergizing.* Beyond giving in or compromising, how can you work with others to develop a solution that is better than anyone might have thought of on their own?
- *Sharpening the saw.* To be effective, you must take care of yourself mentally, physically, spiritually, socially, and emotionally.

Measuring Success for the School: Metrics and Benchmarks

Measuring success begins with the school's mission and values. Everything the school considers doing should be held up against the mission and shared values. The dean and the members of the leadership team must question every major activity and determine whether it aligns with and contributes to the attainment of the mission. He or she should also determine if the activity aligns with the stated values and whether it contributes to the long-term success of the business school or university.

A critical method to measure success begins with the strategic plan for the school. While there are many processes and formats for strategic planning, all of them should provide important detail about goals and metrics, as well as the "how," "who," and "when" of the activity.

- *Goals and objectives.* Ask yourself, what are you seeking to accomplish?
- *Metrics.* How will you measure your success?
- *How.* What tactics and/or action plans will you use to achieve the goal?
- *Who.* What individual(s) will be responsible for implementation? What resources will they require to achieve the stated goal?
- *When.* What is the time frame in which the plan will be implemented and the results assessed?

As a leader, it is vital to let those working with you do their jobs. If you are going to develop your staff and team successfully, it is important to let them develop their own skills as leaders. You should coach, counsel, ask questions, and answer questions, but you should not tell employees how to do their jobs. If you frame your discussions with each person around the five items noted above, you will go a long way toward developing their leadership skills and will move the school forward at the same time. Do not micromanage.

We benchmark our performance against other business schools. Using internally and externally collected data, we compare our performance against both peer and aspirational schools to determine how we stack up on the important variables. We look at output measures such as graduation rates, starting salaries, assurance of learning results, and faculty intellectual contributions and publications, as well as input measures such as faculty salaries, annual operating budgets, endowment levels, and physical facilities.

The Most Challenging Aspects of Being a Business School Dean

When an individual first becomes a dean, the biggest challenge he or she faces is becoming comfortable with the job, which involves truly getting to know the culture of the school. It's also important to fully understand the way the university seeks to achieve its mission through the development of plans, and the implementation and assessment of results of these plans.

A new dean must constantly be learning more about the strengths and weaknesses of the school and learning how the culture of the university manifests itself in day-to-day operations. He or she is then empowered to develop a strategic plan and implementation tactics for the future. These initial elements normally become well-developed in the first few weeks and months in the position. The most significant contribution a dean can make is to lead and manage the strategic planning process and work with others to convert these plans into the day-to-day operational activities of the school. Success does not happen by accident. It results from careful planning and attention to detail in implementation.

As a dean works in the position for a longer period of time, the daily challenges and activities fall into several broad areas:

1. *Developing and fostering excellent relationships with key individuals.* A dean interacts daily with a wide array of individual stakeholders, including but not limited to: the university president, the provost, other deans, associate/assistant deans and academic leaders within the business school, key faculty members, students, corporate

recruiters, alumni, and individuals who serve on advisory councils. A successful dean must work to develop high-trust and collaborative relationships with each of these individuals and groups. It requires effort and focus. It requires the ability to listen empathetically and respond genuinely and directly. It is as much "art" as it is "science." However, almost every successful dean I have ever seen accomplishes this with great skill and often with grace.

2. *Recruiting talent.* It is well documented that there is a growing shortage of business faculty. To overcome this shortage, a dean must be actively involved in attracting and retaining high-quality faculty talent. The dean's role is to present a dynamic vision of the future and offer tangible assurance that the school will achieve its mission and vision. The dean must work tirelessly to create and sustain a culture of collaboration and cooperation among faculty. It is imperative to create a culture that is attractive to faculty candidates.

3. *Retaining faculty talent is equally important.* Each year, other business schools will attempt to lure away your best faculty talent. At times, the issues will involve compensation. At other times, it will revolve around culture, the faculty member's roles and responsibilities, financial and non-financial support for the faculty member's activities and priorities, and other issues. It is important to develop a good working relationship with department heads and faculty members so you can be actively involved in working effectively to retain your top talent.

4. *Securing resources.* Resources are the fuel that sustains all great ideas. Whether at a publicly supported or private university, the need for resources normally far outstrips the actual resources. Securing resources is normally focused on two areas: internal and external. Each university has its own internal resource allocation process. It is imperative that a new dean understand how this process works. This is best learned from those within the business school, from other deans, and from building and nurturing a strong professional relationship with the provost. Each university is different, and one

cannot assume that what was successful at one university will be successful at others. The process will flow from the culture and decision-making groups and mechanisms that are in place. The second source is external or private funding. These funds come from grants and contracts, executive education, continuing education, or other forms of fees for services. External support also comes in the form of charitable gifts from alumni and friends of the business school. These last two forms of support are increasing in importance. If a dean is to be successful, he or she must understand and enjoy the development and fundraising aspects of a business school. Depending on the size, scope, and complexity of the university's and business school's development operation, a business school dean might spend from 10 to 50 percent of his or her available time on external development activities.

5. *Communications.* No matter how much or in what manner a dean tries to communicate, it is never enough or quite the right approach. There are many key stakeholders, both internal and external. Each stakeholder group requires a communications strategy. As business schools have increased in size and complexity throughout the past ten years, it is more difficult for a dean to communicate effectively with faculty and staff. A dean therefore must develop a broad array of strategies and methods to communicate with stakeholders. Of utmost importance, a dean must remember that communication involves both conveying a message and actively listening to what others are saying.

Essential Qualities for Achieving Long-Term Success as a Dean

Each dean is a unique individual, and each business school has its own culture, so there is no universal set of qualities a dean must possess in order to achieve enduring success. I have often heard that the average tenure of a business school dean is about four years. What does it take for a dean to be successful in the long term? There are certain skills and habits that successful long-term deans have in common. During the past several years, I have studied individuals who became successful long-term deans, and I found that they shared the following attributes:

- *Visionary skills.* Successful business school deans possess skills that allow them to work effectively with others to develop a strong vision and strategic plans to achieve the goals for the business school.

- *The ability to attract and retain talent.* Successfully recruiting and retaining talent is a key component in the long-term success of a business school. Successful deans attract individuals who want to be part of the team and work with a particular dean.

- *Strong interpersonal and facilitation skills.* Successful deans must work effectively with a wide variety of stakeholders, which involves getting along with many personality types. This requires exceptional interpersonal skills, especially the ability to listen empathetically and clearly understand what the other person is saying, both verbally and non-verbally. The various stakeholder groups require strong facilitation skills, in which the dean draws out and develops the best ideas from the group.

- *Patience.* Most successful deans have a clear picture of what the successful future looks like and how to achieve the desired results. It is equally important to realize that others will not see the same vision or the means to achieve it. It is imperative to exercise patience, as it will provide the time necessary for others to see and share the vision. It may take a little longer, but in the end, a business school will be more successful when it truly is a shared vision.

- *Humor.* Effective deans frequently display a keen sense of humor. This often manifests itself when a dean uses humor to defuse a tense situation or conflict. Being able to help others see the humor in a situation can be an effective means of moving the group forward toward the desired result.

- *Humility.* Successful deans know everything is not about them as individuals. Successful deans display a visible confidence while simultaneously exhibiting a humility that allows others to step into the spotlight and receive the credit for success. Successful long-term deans are often "servant leaders."

The Biggest Misconceptions of the Role of a Business School Dean

Faculty members often remark that they have no desire to be deans. They enjoy the traditional faculty roles of teaching and research and the time flexibility associated with being a professor. They see a dean's job as an endless stream of meetings, dealing with difficult individuals, engaging the politics of the campus, fighting for resources, meeting alumni, students, parents, and other stakeholders, working long hours, and having to "be on" much of the time. While some of this is true, much of it is a misconception; above all, these notions negate the powerful positives of being a business school dean, a role I believe is the best job on campus.

Serving as a business school dean provides a balance of internal and external focus. While the dean is ultimately responsible for the day-to-day operation of the business school, others are usually much more involved in these functions. Developing and supporting a high-functioning team allows a dean to spend more time on campus-wide activities and off-campus activities, such as alumni relations and fundraising. These functions can include exciting activities such as developing new academic programs, working across the various divisions of the university, raising much-needed private support for the business school, and strategic planning, which involves decisions about where the university will be in five to ten years.

Keeping Your Edge

As the head of an academic institution, it is critical for a dean to be aware of emerging trends and technologies in the industry. Further, given that the average tenure of a business school dean is slightly less than four years, when one exceeds this average, it becomes even more important to keep on top of your game and focused on the things that will help move the school forward. Below are resources and habits that have proven successful tools in maintaining an edge as the dean of a business school:

- *Mentors.* Each of us needs mentors, people to whom we turn for perspective and advice. Sometimes these individuals will be fellow deans, and other times they will not be in this field at all. In any situation, your mentor needs to be someone who can and will give you direct perspective and advice. Seek this type of person out and carefully cultivate the relationship. The relationship will pay huge dividends.

- *New and classic reading material.* There is a wealth of new material written each year. Some publications are trendy; others are timeless. For me, two of the books I always return to are Stephen Covey's, *The 7 Habits of Highly Effective People* and the more recent *The 8th Habit: From Effectiveness to Greatness.* Even though the material is well-known, I always find a new perspective or a way to use the habits to approach an aspect of the job from a different perspective.

- *Redefine your position and priorities.* This was one of the best pieces of advice I received from a business school dean who had served very successfully as the dean of a business school for nearly twenty years. After a few years of focusing on a particular aspect of the position, it can become boring and unfulfilling. Instead of letting the job get the better of you, refocus your time and attention in a new direction. For example, you might become more involved in leading the development of a new master's program or leading the effort to increase private support for the school.

- *Balance your life.* In a dean's position, it is very easy to become swept up in the demands of the job. There is always another person to call, another project to complete, or something as simple as a dozen more e-mails requiring a response. It is critical to your long-term success and health to strike a balance between work and your personal life. It is important to spend quality time with family and friends and keep yourself in good physical, mental, and spiritual health. Each person needs to develop a plan to achieve this balance. No one way is right for all, but it is critical that you find a means that works for you and then stick to your plan.

- *Listen to others.* Ask open-ended questions. As a dean, others are often looking to you for answers. While it may seem easy to answer their questions, this does not readily develop the talents of others. Instead, develop the critical skill of listening to others. What are they really saying? What are they not saying? Beyond the words they use, what are their non-verbal actions and tone of voice telling you? Learn to listen empathetically and ask probing questions. This helps the person find the answers he or she is seeking. This approach is similar to that advocated by the old proverb, "Feed a man a fish, and he will eat for a day. Teach him how to fish, and you'll feed him for a lifetime."

Advice for Heading a Business School

During the course of my career, I have been lucky enough to receive much great advice. Some of this advice came from mentors, while other times it came from individuals I did not even know that well. Perhaps the best advice I ever received was in my first six months as dean. The chairperson of the College of Business Executives' advisory council told me, "Be willing to fail." At the time, these words did not seem that significant to me, but as I reflect back upon the accomplishments this school has achieved, I realize that all of them required calculated risks; the outcome was far from certain, but we were willing to take risks and possibly fail in order to accomplish a great deal. Since then, another person put it best by saying, "If you're not living on the edge, you are taking up too much room."

In turn, the best advice I can give any dean is to listen, be patient, and be assertive of your ideas and position. I will often refer to Stephen Covey's fifth habit: seek first to understand, then to be understood. We often encounter individuals who are upset, concerned, or have strong opinions about an issue. Before you can begin to discuss your perspective with others, it is important that you understand their perspective and how they came to hold their viewpoints. To do so requires empathetic listening and real patience. Many of us want to jump in and state our perspective or position as quickly as possible; however, this approach is unlikely to be successful until the other individual has fully explained his or her perspective. This is not to say you automatically give in to someone else's position. Rather, let the other person explain his or her perspective first and then assertively explain your own.

Changes to the Education Industry over the Past Few Years

Business education is continually becoming more global and entrepreneurial. The growth rate of private, for-profit educational providers is accelerating, and the traditional role of state-supported universities is changing. Distance education and the delivery of educational services are evolving, fostering new ways for business schools to enter markets and compete with other schools.

The competitive landscape for a business school is highly dynamic. It is both stimulating and somewhat uncertain. These changes make for exciting times for business schools to develop distance education, executive and continuing education, certificate programs, and other forms of education programs.

Robert D. Reid is the dean of the College of Business at James Madison University. The College of Business provides bachelor's and master's degree programs for more than 3,800 students. With a team consisting of more than 150 faculty and staff, the College of Business provides exceptional educational opportunities for students. The College of Business faculty has been recognized for excellence in curriculum innovation, especially in the areas of curriculum integration and experiential learning.

Prior to becoming dean in 1996, Dr. Reid was the department head of marketing and hospitality management. While in this role, he held the first J. Willard Marriott Professorship in hospitality and tourism management. Before joining the faculty at James Madison University, he was an associate professor at Virginia Tech.

Dr. Reid has conducted numerous professional workshops and seminars for both public and private organizations. He has consulted with such organizations as the Colonial Williamsburg Foundation, ARAMARK, ITT-Sheraton, R.R. Donnelley, West Virginia University, Volvo-White, Celanese, and the National Restaurant Association.

He has authored or co-authored four editions of Hospitality Marketing Management *and was a contributing author of two other books,* The Practice of

Hospitality Management *and* Introduction to Hotel and Restaurant Management. *Dr. Reid has written or co-authored more than forty journal and professional articles and was a recipient of an "Article of the Year" award presented by the Cornell Hotel and Restaurant Administration Quarterly.*

Dr. Reid has actively served as a leader within numerous professional and civic groups including the International Council on Hotel, Restaurant, and Institutional Management, the Southern Business Administration Association, and Beta Gamma Sigma.

Dedication: *To Susan, for her personality, humor, and positive view of life. And to the many mentors and role models who have helped me throughout my career.*

Maintaining Your Edge and Changing with the Times

Melvin T. Stith

Dean, Whitman School of Management

Syracuse University

The fundamental purpose of business schools in general and the Whitman School in particular is to develop the future business leaders for the global society. As the twenty-first century unfolds, business schools must increasingly emphasize curricula and activities that challenge students to look and think beyond the United States and to operate in an ethical manner. In a competitive field, creating new markets and doing business where there are no competitors is the only way to thrive.

The Whitman School of Management is a student-centered, knowledge-driven school where everyone is encouraged to embrace idea innovation. These days, we are focusing on new collaborative, interdisciplinary programs so our graduates are more competitive in an increasingly global, cross-cultural marketplace. For example, we merged the strategy and human resources department with law and public policy, so students in this realm would have a solid understanding, when dealing with management issues in the marketplace, of ethical and legal boundaries. Another example: into our marketing department, we integrated supply chain management and retail management so our marketing students don't just study brand management. We made that program more interdisciplinary, so now students see the whole interrelatedness of that field, from raw materials to manufacturers to intermediaries (i.e., retailers) to consumers. We believe it is crucial for students to be involved in real-world, relevant experiences as early as possible—through internships, studying abroad, national competitions, and interaction with corporate recruiters who come to campus—so they are truly engaged with and prepared for the work world. All Whitman students are required to have an internship and be involved in service learning. Additionally, the majority of our students have a study abroad experience.

The Dean's Role

My role as dean is to provide vision and strategic thinking that results in establishing objectives and goals, and to offer leadership for everyone in the school and everyone with a vested interest in the school, from current and prospective students and their parents to alumni, the corporate community, and friends.

I have an open door policy as dean. No idea is off the table, and I take everyone's opinion into consideration. Determining what direction to take the school in and how to get there is a tremendous responsibility that I take very seriously. I use the insights of the Whitman faculty and staff, as well as our alumni and corporate partners, in making determinations for the school as a whole. Their input contributes to our understanding of what skills and knowledge base recruiters are seeking in the marketplace, as well as what programs and activities our alumni can best support. I take into account all input from these various audiences and make decisions accordingly, making sure to supply the necessary and appropriate resources to implement and carry out decisions as needed. Appropriate resources include human resources (sufficient and qualified faculty and staff to accomplish tasks at hand and have a vision for the future), technology resources (making sure to stay on top of the latest and best trends that will affect the business world and higher education), and of course financial resources (to fund new initiatives and programs).

My role also includes building strong alliances with alumni and the corporate community and other Whitman friends. I am out in the corporate community and among our alumni a significant amount of time, advocating on behalf of the school with other Syracuse University stakeholders such as the deans of the other schools, the vice chancellor, and the chancellor. This type of advocacy is necessary to let others know the impact business schools can have on the campus and the community. While external stakeholders may not make decisions for the school, they certainly can influence the direction a university can take overall, and it is important for everyone to realize the crucial role business schools have on campus and their influence on the accumulation and allocation of resources. Additionally, I serve on several boards of directors of publicly held companies. I try to create partnerships on campus and off that lead to "win-win" situations.

Overall, my role is to provide an excellent academic environment where people want to come to teach, research, and work; where students want to come to learn; and where alumni are made to feel proud of their alma mater.

Establishing Goals and a Leadership Plan

My goal is to create centers of excellence here at Whitman. Each of our academic departments—accounting, entrepreneurship, finance, general management, and marketing—should be its own best competition in order to make it the best program it can possibly be. This is achieved in large part through faculty. Our faculty members are more than just instructors in the classroom. We aim to recruit and retain prominent thinkers in the business world. At the same time, students come first, so we aim to attract the best mentors for our young people. The outstanding contributions of our faculty in both their fields and in our classrooms make each department a center of excellence.

I also seek to embrace "scholarship in action"—the ambitious mission of Syracuse University, which is to strive for excellence by connecting to ideas, problems, and professions in the world, and to be a university where this excellence is tested in the marketplace. Scholarship in action means getting students out of the classroom and into the local, regional, and international arena to apply their knowledge. We want them to participate in internships—in fact, a number of our students go beyond the one supervised internship requirement and end up doing two or three or four internships, some international. Community service is another example of an important out-of-classroom experience, and Whitman students have consistently been among the most involved in the community among all Syracuse University students. Whitman students help start minority businesses through our South Side Innovation Center and the South Side Connect Project. Some Whitman students spend six weeks in South Africa assisting entrepreneurs to maintain and grow their small businesses. They volunteer to do tax returns for low-income individuals, and they mentor elementary school students through our "Balance the Books" and "Lead 2 Succeed" programs, among others. Other activities include competing in CASE competitions nationwide and even internationally, and the annual Syracuse University-wide Panasci Business Plan Competition that awards more than $40,000 in prize money to the winning business plans. We believe application is fundamental to learning, and we view scholarship in action through a business lens. We believe the business world, infused as it is with high-caliber innovation, enterprising new leaders, and community engagement, has the ability to effect change in our world like no other industry. Ultimately, by embracing this mission, we are preparing our students for a high-tech, global job world where they can distinguish themselves as leaders.

My leadership plan for our school is to develop an engaged and caring community of scholars, staff, and students who always feel connected to Whitman no matter where they are in the world or in their careers. My plan also includes having outstanding students and faculty. In general, business schools need to have strong support from the business and alumni communities because our futures are intertwined with these two groups. The business community grows and innovates due in part to the new professional hires in various companies and industries. These new hires in turn support the initiatives and programs of the schools from which they graduated, and this support makes business schools more competitive, thereby enhancing the ability of graduates (i.e., future hires) to be more innovative and attractive to recruiters.

A Winning Team

No dean can successfully do the job of leading a school on his or her own. It is important to be supported by faculty, staff, students, and alumni who share qualities such as honesty and innovation, and who are willing to engage in honest and open dialogue and to build a caring community.

In my case, I welcome the support and insight of our senior associate dean, who as "second in command" at the school helps set the agenda, as well as oversees the work of faculty, the Career Center, the information technology department, and the undergraduate program. Externally, the executive associate dean for institutional advancement leads an exemplary team that builds and maintains important relationships with many significant Whitman alumni.

Additional invaluable support comes from the entire management committee of the school, consisting of the department chairs. This team of individuals defines the mission and direction of the school and both individually and collectively strives to achieve our goals. I have daily informal meetings with the associate deans and many of the directors at Whitman to discuss strategy and implementation. We hold monthly deans and directors meetings, monthly management committee meetings, as well as a semiannual management committee retreat. We also hold a semiannual meeting with the Whitman corporate advisory council. The council has been an invaluable asset in providing guidance, access, and support for Whitman.

Benchmarks for Success

I measure success in a multitude of ways:

1. *Recruiting and retention of high-quality faculty.* Whitman strives to be a center of research and instruction where reputable and prominent thinkers in the business school world want to work. By recruiting and retaining excellent faculty, we are ensuring that Whitman is succeeding in contributing valid perspectives to various fields in the business world, and that through these contributions, outstanding graduate students will choose to study here for their M.B.A.s and Ph.Ds. Benchmarks include faculty publications and excellence in research and teaching, and the quantity and quality of the institutes who try to hire our faculty away.

2. *Support and involvement of alumni.* We strive to provide our students with the best possible educational experience and, therefore, measure our success by their continued involvement with the school upon their graduation, whether it is through welcoming our students to their places of business as interns, by returning to campus as guest speakers, by supporting the efforts of the school through donations, or by being advocates for Whitman in their communities and professions.

3. *Placement of students.* We seek to build and maintain strong relationships with corporate recruiters in order to ensure that our students have the most opportunities available to them upon graduation. We measure our placement rate both quantitatively and qualitatively and view our students' professional success as an extension of our own. Benchmarks include the number of students who are gainfully employed within six months of graduation and how they are promoted or advanced in their careers.

4. *Satisfaction of current students.* At Whitman, students come first. We seek to build strong relationships with each and every incoming freshman, transfer, and graduate student that will span not only their time in our classrooms but the rest of their lives. We measure student satisfaction through annual surveys, monthly meetings, student participation on school committees and in school clubs and organizations, and our open door policy.

5. *Recruiting and retention of high-quality students.* Whitman is ranked in the top fifty for all undergraduate business programs nationwide, and we have been nationally recognized for both our entrepreneurship and supply chain management programs. We know we are doing exceptional work with exceptional individuals—having the outside validation only means we will continue to attract highly qualified and dedicated students. As the Millennial Generation continues to enter higher education institutes, so will Whitman continue to offer the programs and services these technologically savvy, group-oriented, ethnically diverse, and future-focused young people expect and demand.

6. *High-quality faculty, staff, and administrators.* Many times, staff and administrators are the first contact with students, alumni, corporate recruiters, and prospective students. Maintaining outstanding staff and administrators goes hand-in-hand with maintaining the outstanding work of the Whitman School as a whole. We offer a number of incentives to maintain quality faculty, including favorable teaching assignments, an advanced technology environment for learning and academic research, financial support to conduct research, summer stipends, and sabbaticals, as well as fostering a collegial environment.

There are four key strategies that can help ensure that a business school will continue to grow successfully. First, directly engage the alumni community through alumni events, athletic events, internship fairs, and lecture series. I also meet with alumni in their professional work environments, and we encourage select alumni to be part of the Whitman advisory council and the University-wide board of trustees. Second, make sure the business school is perceived as an integral part of the campus. For these last two points, we make sure to market ourselves strategically among these audiences. We publicize all of our events to alumni and campus-wide, making sure these groups know the events are open to the public. We place stories in the university newspaper and in the student-run campus newspaper. We created and disseminate two HTML e-newsletters (one sent out monthly, the other semi-monthly) that update alumni and select campus audiences about our activities, accomplishments, and events. We also distribute our annual report to alumni. Third, work with the corporate community to gain and maintain support of your school. Our Career Center and institutional advancement staff work hard to conduct visits to the corporate community and to build relationships with key recruiters. The Career Center distributes a third HTML e-newsletter to constituents that updates them on important announcements and events. Fourth, maintain an open door policy where the barriers of "the office of the dean" can be broken down. This policy is explicit in every message I send to faculty, students, staff, and alumni—from the regular HTML e-newsletters we send to these various audiences, to public addresses I make, to welcome announcements located on the LCD screens around our school.

Overcoming Challenges

The business school dean faces five key challenges: recruiting the best and brightest students; maintaining a competitive scholarship fund to attract the most in-demand students, especially at the graduate level; retaining the best and brightest faculty; maintaining a fair and equitable salary structure for all faculty, staff, and administrators; and maintaining a cutting-edge and technologically advanced facility to support faculty research and service. These challenges are overcome by offering competitive teaching assignments and opportunities to teach extra courses for pay, as well as by providing endowed positions with salary supplements, advanced technology in every classroom and in faculty suites, and funding for research projects and attendance at professional meetings.

In order to overcome these challenges and work well with others, deans need to be good listeners. They need to be willing to engage and discuss different ideas and viewpoints. They need to be honest, open, and fair with all people. They need to avoid political agendas where some people think they have special access to the dean and others do not. Deans need to be willing to confront challenging issues head on and bring closure to those issues. They need to make tough decisions and share with everyone why and how those decisions were made.

The biggest misconception about deans is that they have little or no power; in fact, they have an enormous influence over faculty, staff, and students and can use their powers of persuasion to help their institution thrive.

How to Succeed

In order to keep my edge and succeed in my role as dean, I try to participate in external activities related to academe as often as possible. These activities include serving on peer review teams; attending seminars hosted by executive firms; talking regularly with people in the industry about what skills are needed so our students can get the best jobs; and serving on corporate boards. The most useful resource is human: I rely on good human resources, including having the best staff and an administrative team I trust, people who want to work at Whitman and who do an excellent job moving the school forward.

I also try to spend as much time as I can with faculty, staff, and students. Being around students as much as I can cuts down the barrier of "the office of the dean," so there are more occasions for open dialogue. I keep an open door policy, and I seek to engage students in social settings where they feel comfortable and want to talk. When I can, I eat in the same café where our students eat. I go to the same athletic events. I visit them in their classrooms. I socialize with them at Whitman events like our annual International Day. Being visible and accessible is the best strategy for success as a dean.

Feedback is also very important. Every three years, a major review of the dean is conducted by the faculty. I am evaluated on the enhancement of Whitman's reputation and rankings, student retention and placement, alumni involvement with Whitman, and the accomplishment of annual goals. Additionally, our corporate advisory council is open and honest and offers guidance about the direction of the school and how our leadership can best fulfill the school's promise. I meet with people in small groups or in a one- on- one session to talk about issues of concern. E-mails and other types of electronic communications, such as our semi-monthly "Dean's Update" HTML e-newsletter, have assisted with this process.

The role of the business school dean has increasingly become much more external than it has been traditionally. Far less time is spent dealing with academic issues; those issues are left to the senior associate dean. Deans must now spend the bulk of their time building their external brand, as well as connecting with alumni, the corporate community, and other university stakeholders. I believe the role of the dean will become even more external in the years to come. Deans will increasingly spend far less time on classroom teaching, if any. The change in the role of dean has come about because of the increased need for deans to provide additional resources to support programs and activities. Regular budget allocations from central administration cannot provide enough funds to build an exemplary business school. Therefore, the dean must turn to external audiences—alumni, foundations, and the corporate community—to provide the necessary funds to build and maintain a quality program. Professional schools must seek professional appointments for their graduates. Therefore, the dean must build a strong relationship with the corporate community to ensure that graduates are hired and hired well. I believe the changes have had a positive effect and have forced deans to become engaged with the real world and practice what we preach to our students.

Business School Leadership Philosophy

I often give advice that is based upon the way I was raised—value the work you do. Work hard and surround yourself with good people and good mentors—these are crucial components to achieving any kind of success in life. Trust people you work with to do the right thing. My good friend Jim Moran says, "The future belongs to those who prepare for it." I often give this advice to others and mind it myself by preparing for the future.

I have three golden rules for running a business school successfully:

1. Be approachable and be a good listener.
2. Let people know and believe you are fair and honest, and exhibit those qualities every day.
3. Engage in meaningful dialogue with everyone.

Generating Income

Business schools, like all universities, must constantly look for ways to generate revenue in order to pay faculty salaries; meet capital expenditures to create modern facilities; invest in new technology; and maintain scholarships for outstanding undergraduates and to attract graduate students to campus.

Whitman, like many others, generates income through executive programs and special programs for the corporate community and alumni. In general, our external programs are a result of the needs of our alumni and others in the corporate community who seek to have short-term programs that advance or refresh skills. Endowment is built through support from key constituencies such as parents, foundations, corporations, alumni, and other special friends. At Syracuse University, the money is invested by an investment committee established by the university's board of trustees that make decisions entirely independent of the Whitman School.

Fundraising

At our school, the long-term goals for fundraising are to: (1) create centers of excellence out of each of our academic departments; (2) create endowed professorships and chairs for faculty; (3) create endowed fellowships and scholarships for deserving students; (4) build and maintain a capital improvement fund; (5) build and maintain a technology fund; (6) build and maintain a fund for special purposes (for example, when financial aid-based students have the opportunity but not the resources to study abroad, and other unique opportunities that will enhance the students' educational experiences); and (7) build and maintain a faculty research fund to support valid and potentially influential research by faculty that will lead to publication in a well-respected, peer-reviewed journal appropriate to their field.

My process for philanthropy is to set an expectation of value early on and then meet that expectation. The alumni and friends of our school have come to expect great things from the school, and we have aimed to deliver on those expectations. This forms a bond that lasts a lifetime and can potentially reap great rewards—both monetarily and otherwise—for the school.

The Importance of External Rankings

External rankings play a role in attracting good students and good faculty. In the end, it is what happens inside the school, away from the rankings, that matters, and that is dependent on dedicated leadership, sufficient resources, and relevant curricula. At Whitman, we already know we are doing good work—when we are recognized for this by an external ranking, it only validates what we're already confident of. Although we take rankings seriously and they are important to us, we ultimately do not judge ourselves by the rankings.

Planning for the Future

Technology and online learning is a very interesting and strong new segment in business education. Whitman has an exemplary online M.B.A. program and is introducing an online M.S. in accounting. We will continue to look at this segment to offer short-term programs. Our programs will remain unique in that they all have a residency component, so these students can come to campus and we can connect with them and include them as part of the Whitman community. There are no drawbacks to these programs, but the challenge is to maintain a cutting-edge technological environment and make sure the professors are appropriate for teaching in this delivery system.

As our school continues its move into the future, I plan on holding strategic sessions with key stakeholders and subsequently developing documents everyone will review and react to. These documents will include the departmental plans and goals for various Whitman centers (the Bennett Center for Tax Research, the Snyder Innovation Center, and the Kiebach Center for International Business Studies, among others). From those reactions, I will develop a strategic plan that will be under continuous reconstruction, as I and other Whitman stakeholders are always looking for ways to improve what we do and how we do it. The strategic plan becomes a dynamic roadmap on how Whitman will implement and achieve our strategic objectives.

Melvin T. Stith is dean of the Martin J. Whitman School of Management at Syracuse University. Mr. Stith returned to his alma mater in January of 2005 to become the sixteenth dean of the Whitman School of Management. From 1991 to November of 2004, he was dean and the Jim Moran professor of business administration in the College of Business at Florida State University in Tallahassee, and previously he was associate professor and chair of the department of marketing at Florida State. He was a visiting professor in the School of Business and Industry at Florida A&M University from 1982 to 1985, and associate dean and assistant professor in the College of Business at the University of South Florida from 1977 to 1982.

Mr. Stith has shared his research expertise as a consultant or lecturer for many private companies and public agencies, including the Dracket Company, American Hospital Supply, Florida Department of Education, Florida Department of Transportation, Glembys, Fireman's Fund Insurance Co., Anheuser-Busch, Kent Publishing Co., JM Family Enterprises, Associated Credit Bureaus, and the University of Wisconsin. He is also active in the Ph.D. Project, a national foundation that works to recruit black, Hispanic, and American Indian students to the business school professoriate.

A Vietnam veteran, Mr. Stith served in the U.S. Army Military Intelligence Command from 1968 to 1971, and achieved the rank of captain during his military tenure. A native of Jarratt, Virginia, he received his undergraduate education at Norfolk State University and his M.B.A. and Ph.D. in marketing from the Whitman School of Management at Syracuse University. He serves on the board of Flowers Food Inc., the Graduate Management Admissions Council, and Synovus Financial Corporation.

Surviving the Marathon

Lynne Richardson

Dean, Miller College of Business

Ball State University

The Dean's Role

In my mind, the dean of the business school holds one of the premiere positions on campus. The dean helps formulate and execute strategy, works with some of the smartest people at the university, and develops relationships with many external constituents, from parents to recruiters to alumni. Days are long, with many appointments filling the calendar, but life is rarely dull. A typical day might include meetings with my leadership team in the college, interactions with individual faculty members or students to discuss issues of interest to them, and engagements elsewhere on campus or in the community. There are probably several phone calls to alumni and/or donors throughout the day and lots of computer time writing reports or responding to e-mails. And all of this is before the department chair shows up at my door with an "emergency." Emergencies are certainly not routine, but they happen more often than I prefer. Emergencies we have dealt with include a faculty member who had a heart attack and would be out an extended period of time and a senior administrator demanding something yesterday. It certainly keeps life interesting. Your best-laid plans (because you *do* practice time management) just went out the window.

One of the more important tasks confronting a dean is the appointment of the business school leadership team. Within the dean's office, I look for associate deans who would complement my skill set, have a positive attitude about change, have academic administration experience, and can be customer-oriented to all of our customers. While the faculty elects the department chairs, it is important for each of them to understand that this job is not a popularity contest; tough decisions will be made and the chair must have thick skin. No one in academic administration is universally liked, because you cannot please all of the people all of the time. Awareness of this on the front end certainly prepares you for those days when it is "you against the world."

My college's leadership team is composed of the dean, two associate deans, and an assistant to the dean, plus five department chairs. The associate deans have specific roles: one manages our instruction (teaching) and operations, and the other's responsibilities are for research and outreach. The assistant to the dean manages our student services area for both graduate and undergraduate students.

For a dean to have long-term success, he or she must continue listening, learning, and revitalizing himself or herself. This will, of course, mean different things to different people, and at varying rates. There are successful business school deans who have passed the twenty-year mark, while others struggle to surpass a year. Most deans, upon their appointment, determine their three-to-five-year agenda in consultation with the faculty and other stakeholders. They put their leadership team in place, determine the right strategies for implementing the agenda, and then the train leaves the station. At some point, much of the work is done and the dean has run out of steam. Then what happens? Deans who serve long periods tell me they must revitalize themselves. Sometimes this means embracing a new focus (e.g., global work, Association for the Advancement of Collegiate Schools of Business International (AACSB) accreditation work, and consulting), but many of them switch deanships. There are AACSB-accredited business school deans serving their fifth school. I have often said I want to leave the deanship when people are still sorry to see me go. Personally, I try to attend AACSB conferences in which I learn about new topics and gain ideas that can be implemented in my college. Several years ago, I attended the Harvard M.L.E. program, which, as much as anything, helped me understand how others on campus think (the program involves individuals at approximately the same level on campus interacting for two weeks).

Challenges

The most challenging aspects I see for the business school dean are making sure we have the resources (financial, human, and facilities) to educate our students, and motivating faculty to change when necessary. Networking to identify prospects for fundraising is important for increasing financial resources, and ongoing discussions with the university's administration are required for the human and facilities concerns. As more business faculty hit retirement age, we are realizing that current faculty salaries are not sufficient to recruit new Ph.Ds. My job is to make sure we have the resources to entice the faculty we want to our school. We offer faculty competitive teaching loads with a fair number of students (our faculty teach three courses per semester, but the total number of students tends to average approximately 100 per semester), with at least one stipend for a guaranteed summer of research. We also have a Bureau of Business Research, a resource many of our long-term faculty take for granted. There is an editor and statistician in the bureau who assists faculty with their research. This is a tremendous selling point for recruiting new faculty. All new faculty also get a graduate assistant.

Motivating faculty to change is probably the biggest challenge I face. One example occurred early in my deanship regarding integration of our business core curriculum. Like many business schools, we were teaching principles of every business discipline, followed by courses in the major subject, with a capstone course in business strategy. The idea, as I understand it, was that students in the capstone course would have an "aha" moment and would then understand how the business disciplines are integrated. We all know it just does not work that way. So I challenged our faculty to figure out a way to address this problem.

To jumpstart the process, I asked an administrator from a business school that had radically changed how they did their undergraduate business core to visit us and share their story. On the front end, I told the faculty this was an extreme example of change. I was not expecting something this radical, but I wanted them to see what could be done if faculty worked together. Frankly, the other school's plan scared my group to death, so they immediately began considering a variety of models. It took about eighteen months of research and discussions, but the faculty has now embraced a new model (using a common case in all core classes) to address integration. The common case allows us to use examples and require assignments built on the same company in all core business classes. The idea is that students will hear the same company name and become so familiar with the case that they will start integrating the business functions on their own. Our faculty created the assignments that are being used in the core classes (e.g., no matter what marketing section a student is in, the professor in that section will require the same assignment related to the case).

The company the case focuses on has partnered with us, and the faculty members are thrilled with our new direction. We are doing assessment to make sure students are learning what we want them to learn, and it is working. What I learned from this process was that for real change to occur and endure, the faculty must drive it. The dean cannot dictate change.

Facing Change

The role of dean is evolving. As recently as ten years ago, most deans were more of insiders. Today's dean must spend considerable amounts of time externally. This makes it a balancing issue. If you have developed the right leadership team, the dean should be free to spend time outside of the university, friend-raising and fundraising. But the faculty still wants to see the dean. Ways I have tried to bridge the gap are by having monthly faculty lunches and a weekly internal newsletter. Once a year, faculty members are invited to an unstructured lunch with me so they can have direct access without having to come to the dean's office. The newsletter has been a big hit, especially among faculty who join us from other institutions in which they didn't have such a thing. The newsletter resulted from my realization that all of my department chairs did not communicate equally. With the newsletter (which I personally write), all faculty and staff have access to the same information. We use it to highlight good works of faculty and staff, share decisions that have been made at the college level by the leadership team, and profile upcoming events. We also do "TGIFs" on Friday afternoons, following the monthly college research colloquium. TGIFs are truly social events designed to bring faculty and staff together to have fun and get to know one another. We've had magicians join us, faculty have shared their karaoke talents, and teams have competed to win scavenger hunts in the building. With budgets continuing to be tight, I can only speculate that deans will be expected to raise even more money externally in upcoming years.

How do I keep my edge as a dean? I can think of several ways. First, my relationship with my advisory board motivates me to keep going every day. When things are not going well internally, I can talk to a member of my board and be encouraged to "stay the course." Second, I try to attend AACSB conferences to learn what other schools are doing and then try to incorporate the best practices I see into what we are doing at my school. The network of deans you develop is important for "therapy sessions." Additionally, I attempt to communicate well with my faculty and staff. If a majority of them do not agree with our direction, I cannot be an effective dean. I also think it is important to take your vacations every year. I know too many people who are workaholics and really never give themselves a chance to charge their batteries. Vacations are downtime for me, and I return from them with renewed energy and brimming with ideas.

Advice for Business School Deans

One of the best pieces of advice I received early in my deanship was to remember that this job really is a marathon, not a sprint. My first year, I had a big agenda and, while we accomplished many of our agenda items, my lone associate dean and I were exhausted by May. The president of the university reminded me late that spring of the advice above, and it has helped me put things in perspective and keep some balance in my life. If you let it, this job will consume you to the exclusion of all else. As a working mom with a supportive spouse, I find that trying to remember that "work will still be here tomorrow" is a good mantra.

I share that same advice with others, especially about the balance. I know many deans who have had stress-related illnesses because they have not learned to put the job in perspective to the rest of their lives. Also, I remind my department chairs that they did not become administrators to become more popular. I expect them to make the appropriate decision regarding situations, and not necessarily the popular one. That is a hard one for many people to swallow. Thick skin is a requirement of this job.

My three golden rules for being a dean would include: (1) be transparent as much as you can; (2) do the right thing, even when it means others will not like your decision; and (3) communicate, communicate, communicate— especially to your faculty and staff and to external audiences (alumni, advisory boards, and friends of the college). A dean needs to enjoy his or her work. If the job is not fun most days, he or she should find something else to do, because chances are, he or she is not an effective dean.

Acquiring Funds

Depending on the university's structure, business schools can make money through executive education programs (e.g., executive M.B.A.s, certificate programs, and customized courses), grants and contracts, and fundraising. Every university is different with regard to revenue generation. We tend to generate the most money at my university through fundraising, with occasional grants and contracts. Our executive education program is funneled through the School of Extended Education. While faculty are compensated for participating in programs, the business school does not receive funds.

Hands down, the most expensive element of operating a business school is the payroll. With faculty salaries skyrocketing (with no end in sight because of large numbers of retirements expected in the next ten years and fewer seats in Ph.D. programs around the United States), payroll will continue to drive the business school budget. Making sure technology and facilities are up to date is an expensive proposition as well, but generally these are not driving the annual budget.

We build our school's endowment through fundraising. Our university's foundation then invests our money for us, and its board determines the annual payout (generally driven by the stock market's performance). For the most part, our long-term goals for endowed dollars center on scholarships, professorships (to attract and retain excellent faculty), and supporting start-up ventures in our college. Our goal is to have some seed money so faculty can create new centers, commercial ventures, and so on. Typically, faculty drive new ideas in a college, and the dean's role is to help make new ventures happen.

Ideally, to effectively fundraise, my director of development and I sit down after talking to a variety of stakeholders and create a wish list of priorities for our school. Then we prospect for donors who might have an interest in investing in these priorities. I cannot overemphasize the friend-raising that must occur before you can expect an effective fundraising campaign. People give to people and so, for me to approach someone about making a gift, I must have a relationship with them. Many hours are spent getting to know prospective donors (alumni, friends of the school, businesses, foundations) before an ask is made. While some gifts occur out of the blue (our college's naming gift was an estate gift from an alumnus who, unknowingly to the university, had us in his will), most are more systematic. While many private universities fundraise well, many of the public universities are just beginning to get organized in this area. We can learn a lot from the incredibly successful campaigns of private universities.

External rankings are a reality business schools must deal with, whether deans like it or not. The university administration, parents, prospective students, and alumni especially like to tout their school's success in this area. The challenge in "playing the rankings game" is that perhaps you lose sight of why we are here: to educate people who have an interest in business. If you focus first on the content of our programs, share that content and what it means to students with your public, and (and it is a big "and") the public thinks what you are doing is exceptional or noteworthy, rankings will probably come. In our school, we try to remember that our programs for students are what is important and, since we do something in one of our programs (entrepreneurship) that no other undergraduate institution does (students risk their graduation every spring by how well they perform in a new venture creation course), we market that, and voters think it noteworthy enough to rank us highly. Our entrepreneurship program is ranked number six in the 2007 *U.S. News & World Report* for undergraduate programs.

For our institution, other things that draw students include our smaller class sizes (at a campus with more than 18,000 students), the personal attention received from the professors, and our experiential learning opportunities. We really emphasize that students can have a small school feel here with all the accoutrements of a larger university.

Obviously, technology and online learning have changed the face of education over the past ten years or so. Online learning has allowed many place-bound or otherwise constrained people who desire a college education to receive one. It has changed the way professors teach and, with the newer technologies evolving, will continue to do so. I can remember earlier in my career having conversations about the potential "end of the traditional university experience." I daresay that will never happen, primarily because college is about more than just what you learn in class (I definitely want my children to experience college in a traditional setting), but certainly we do things differently than we did just a few years ago. Many faculty have resisted the movement to online classes, but others have enthusiastically embraced it. A challenge for business school leaders is to help the faculty determine what its thrusts are to be and, if online (or video-streaming, etc.) is in the mix, make sure the quality delivered through this alternative method is on par with the traditional classroom experience.

Lynne Richardson (Ph.D., University of Alabama) is dean of the Miller College of Business at Ball State University. Previously, she served as associate dean for undergraduate programs and external relations at the University of Alabama at Birmingham.

Ms. Richardson is a member of the Association for the Advancement of Collegiate Schools of Business International board of directors and recently completed a term on the Beta Gamma Sigma board of governors.

Appendices

CONTENTS

APPENDIX A

MEMORANDUM REGARDING ESTIMATION OF THE FINANCIAL CONTRIBUTION TO THE UNIVERSITY BY THE BUSINESS SCHOOL

Business School
YOUR UNIVERSITY

MEMORANDUM

To: Provost/VPAA

From: Dean of the Business School

Re: Estimation of the Financial Contribution to the University by the Business School

Date: July 2, 20XX

Recently you requested that the deans make an assessment of their schools 20XX-XY financial impact in the University. My estimate of the Business School's contribution in 20XX-XY is attached. The estimates include the financial impact of the undergraduate business program and the M.B.A. program on the University's financial status.

A description of the development of the estimates is also included in the attachment. I believe that the estimates provide us with a fairly good set of "ball park" figures, i.e., there may be some errors or things left out but the magnitudes are essentially correct.

Commentary

<u>Overall Impact</u>

In 20XX-XY, the Business School brought in about $5.15 million of revenue on courses in the School alone. The direct costs to operate the Business School amounted to about $2.95 million (in the estimates B + D or $2.43 + $0.52 million in the attachment). Overall, the Business School produced a net contribution to the University of about $2.2 million. For every $1 in revenues directly related to the School, the University got a net of 43 cents toward the coverage of indirect and overhead costs of the University.

Undergraduate Program

The undergraduate business program was directly connected with about $3.46 million in revenues. However, this figure understates the importance of the School because most of the undergraduate business students would be at another university if we did not have the undergraduate business program. Furthermore, the existence of the SBA also produces undergraduate student revenues related to required general education courses that they take, electives that they take outside of business, books that they buy, room and board that they buy from Monmouth, and so forth. Those non-SBA tuition and fees revenues would be realized by other colleges and universities if we did not have the BSBA program.

The cost of instruction that was directly related to the undergraduate business program was approximately $1.65 million. The undergraduate program made a gross contribution to the School and the University of about $1.81 million or 52 cents per dollar of revenue (1.81/3.46).

MBA Program

Virtually all MBA students would have gone elsewhere if we did not have the MBA program. The MBA program produced about $1.69 million in revenues in 20XX-XY. The direct costs of instruction were roughly $0.78 million. The gross margin produced by the MBA program was about $0.91 million. For every $1 of revenue from the MBA program the University gets a net of 53 cents (0.91/1.69 = .53) toward covering indirect School and University costs.

The Importance of Summer School

Summer school is quite profitable for the University and should be included in any analysis of the contribution of the Business School to the

University's financial success. Business School courses produced a gross margin of about $550,000 (revenues less instructor's fees) in fiscal 20XX-XY. The University gets a net profit of about 76 cents ($0.72 million revenue - $0.17 cost million/$0.72 million revenue = .76) on each dollar of revenue for business courses in the summer. Twenty percent of the gross margin produced by the Business School in fiscal year 20XX-XY was due to summer school classes while only 14 percent of the revenues came from summer school.

Twenty-two percent of the MBA credit hours and revenues were generated in the summer sessions of fiscal 20XX-XY. This is worth mentioning since it appears that summer school operations are overlooked in assessments of the MBA program's impact on the University's financial well-being. The undergraduate business courses also make a nice contribution to the University in the summer.

Business School
20XX-XY
Estimated Financial Contribution to Your University
($Millions)

	REVENUES	Undergraduate	Graduate	Totals	
	Spring & Fall Tuition Fees	$2.93 0.18	$1.24 0.08	$4.17 0.26	
	Subtotals	$3.11	$1.32	$4.43	
	Summer School Tuition Fees	$0.33 0.02	$0.34 0.03	$0.67 0.05	
	Subtotals	$0.35	$0.27	$0.72	
(A)	TOTALS	**$3.46**	**$1.69**	**$5.15**	*100%*
	$Dollars Credit Hours	*67%* *77%*	*33%* *23%*	*100%* *100%*	
	COSTS **Instruction** Spring & Fall Summer	 $1.56 0.09	 $0.70 0.08	 $2.26 0.17	
(B)	Subtotals	$1.65	$0.78	$2.43	
(C)	GROSS MARGINS [C = A - B]	$1.81	$0.91	$2.72	*53%*
	$Dollars	*67%*	*33%*	*100%*	
(D)	Other Costs (Admin., Staff, non- compensation costs)			$0.52	*10%*
(E)	TOTAL CONTRIBUTION [E = C – D]			**$2.20**	*43%*

Computations Used in Estimating Business School Related Revenues, Costs and Allocation of Costs

REVENUES

<u>Undergraduate</u>

<u>Fall + Spring 20XX-XY</u>

Tuition and prorated state allocations, if any:
B-School cr. hrs x \$384/cr. hr. x 0.75 discount = \$2,933,280

Fees :
B-School cr.hrs./15 cr. hr. per stu. x \$265/stu. = \$179,935

<u>Summer Sessions</u>

Tuition and prorated state allocations, if any:
B-School cr. hrs. x \$384/cr. hr.:   SS-III, 1996 = \$79,488
                                     SS-I, 1997 = \$245,376

Fees :
Headcount/1.5 courses per stu. x \$130/stu.
                    Summer I = \$5,980
                    Summer II = \$18,460

<u>Graduate</u>

<u>Fall + Spring 20XX-XY</u>

Tuition and prorated state allocations, if any:
B-School cr. hrs. x \$419/cr. hr. = \$1,242,754

Fees :
B-School cr. hrs./5 cr. hr. ave./stu/term x \$130 = \$77,090

Summer Sessions

Tuition and prorated state allocations, if any:
B-School cr. hrs. x $419/cr. hr.: Summer I = $163,410
Summer II = $183,522

Fees :
B-School cr. hrs./1.5 courses/student x $130/student
Summer I = $11,180
Summer II = $12,610

COSTS

Instruction

Fall + Spring

B-School Full-Time Faculty Salaries = $1,629,155
Allocated to undergraduate and graduate programs by percentage of sections taught by full-time faculty for each program (68.8% undergraduate or $1,120,859 and 31.2% graduate or $508,296)

B-School Part-time faculty salaries = $94,000
Number of sections x $2,000 per section, split according to whether the section was a graduate section or an undergraduate section (undergraduate = $72,000 and graduate = $22,000).

Total of salaries related to F/T + P/T faculty times 33% fringe benefits rate = $537,621
(Split-out: undergraduate = $369,883; graduate = $167,738)

Above Totals split-out were: undergraduate = $1,562,742
graduate = $ 698,024

Summers: Summer I & Summer II 20XX-XY

Number of sections x $3,900 per section split by undergraduate and graduate sections = $128,700 (undergraduate $70,200 and graduate $58,500)

Add number of independent studies x $130 each and split according to undergraduate or graduate related course (only a total of $1,820).

Add to each faculty payments figures 33% for fringe benefits.

Above totals split-out were:　　　undergraduate = $93,366
graduate = $78,805

Other Costs

Combination of:

Stipends for chairs	$31,600
Admin. & Staff Salaries	$220,120
Fringe benefits (above x .33)	$83,068
graduate assistantships	$21,690
all other costs (travel, supplies, duplicating, etc.)	$165,000
	$521,478

Courtesy of Dr. William A. Dempsey, Radford University

APPENDIX B

MEMORANDUM REGARDING CALCULATING FINANCIAL CONTRIBUTION OF BUSINESS SCHOOL

Business School
YOUR UNIVERSITY

MEMORANDUM

To: Deans of Other Schools or Colleges

From: Business School Dean

Copy: Provost/VPAA

Re: Calculating Financial Contribution of Business School

Date: July 2, 20XY

I prepared an estimate of the fiscal year 20XX-XY financial contribution of the Business School. You may find it interesting and perhaps helpful to you as an example of how one can estimate revenues, costs, and contributions to the University by a school.

The Business School estimates are easier to make than would be the case for Arts and Sciences since most of the credit hours in business courses are taken by business students in the undergraduate and graduate business programs.

The importance of the Business School is somewhat underestimated in my figures. First, I did not lay claim to revenues related to business students taking courses outside the business school or the revenues from business students for such things as books purchased in the bookstore, room and board fees, and other such revenues. Second, and on the other hand, I did not exclude the credit hours taught to non-business students in business courses which slightly inflates the Business School figures. The net effect of the first and second items combined still underestimates the importance of the Business School.

More sophisticated estimates could be produced that would show to what extent a unit of the University was producing credit hours for other schools or colleges versus credit hours for its own majors.

Courtesy of Dr. William A. Dempsey, Radford University

APPENDIX C

STRATEGIC PLAN

FROM EXCELLENCE TO GREATNESS

ASCENT TO THE TOP:

THE PLAN FOR 2006–2011

JUNE 2006

EXECUTIVE SUMMARY

Over the last eight years, the Smith School has made a remarkable transformation from a very good regional school to a top research and teaching institution offering a wide range of products and services on four continents. The capabilities of our faculty, the scale and quality of our facilities, and the quality of our students have soared so that it is difficult to project back in a linear fashion to trace the school's origins. The Smith School is now at the beginning of another transformation. This transformation will carry the school from excellence to greatness with the following mission:

> *To ascend to one of the top global business schools as measured by the school's stature in research and teaching, and the quality and placement of its students. We will provide a superb research and teaching environment for our faculty and students as well as give our students a first class return on investment for their time and expense.*

The school's strategy ranges from initiatives aimed at producing research and program greatness to initiatives to build the Smith community, technology, brand, and revenues. Within this strategy the school will accomplish the following:

- Continue to recruit internationally recognized faculty stars and continue key hires of senior faculty with leading research records.

- Design and implement the Smith Undergraduate Fellows Program. Introduce the Smith Freshman/Sophomore Fellows Program in AY 2006/07 and the Smith Junior/Senior Fellows Program in AY2007/08 so that all students will be able to participate in at least one Fellows track.
- Continue building the Smith Community of students, faculty, alumni, and recruiters—integrating activities of student, alumni and mentoring programs.
- Improve the school's governance system, accountability and reporting systems, and committee and organizational structures to stimulate the development of the Smith Community, marketing efforts, program delivery and operational efficiencies.
- Fully develop our international partnerships and offer intercontinental opportunities in Asia, Europe and the United States for undergraduate, EMBA and MBA students. Develop a joint degree program in India and identify additional operating locations to extend our global presence.
- Continue to extend technological capabilities so that the school can project its presence everywhere it operates. Ensure that potential users are aware of these capabilities and trained in their use.
- Expand the school's communications, marketing and branding activities through the increased use of traditional, video and Web-based media.
- Plan, design and construct the Annex to Van Munching Hall with targeted occupancy in AY 2007/08 and continue to provide the most advanced technological infrastructure among leading business schools.
- Increase overall revenues for the school so that by 2011 the school has total revenues among the top three public business schools.

Is this strategy achievable? We believe it is. Today, the Smith School's reputation extends around the globe. Graduate and executive programs in China, Europe and Africa have established the school as a truly world class institution. At home, many of our academic areas have been recognized among the top 10-15 in their respective fields. As our reputation grows, so too does our ability to attract leading scholars.

VISION

The extraordinary technological developments of the last decade are spawning new models of competition and economic engagement. Fueled by worldwide information networks, the fundamentals of business are being transformed in every market, in every industry, in every nation. The rapidity and volatility of technical knowledge and market changes require leaders of global businesses who are highly adaptive and receptive to new and complex networks and supply chains of products, systems and information flows. Like businesses, business schools in the new millennium must transform their knowledge and research base, their curricula, and modes of delivery. At the Smith School, we are in the midst of this transformation, with a vision of becoming a model for business education and knowledge advancement for the 21st century.

Over the last eight years, the Smith School has made a remarkable transformation from a very good regional school to a top research and teaching institution offering a wide range of products and services on four continents. The capabilities of our faculty, the scale and quality of our facilities, and the quality of our students have soared so that it is difficult to project back in a linear fashion to trace the school's origins. The Smith School is now at the beginning of another transformation. This transformation will carry the school from excellence to greatness with the mission:

> *To ascend to one of the top global business schools as measured by the school's stature in research and teaching, and the quality and placement of its students. We provide a superb research and teaching environment for our faculty and students as well as give our students a first class return on investment for their time and expense.*

The stature of the Robert H. Smith School of Business has advanced dramatically over the last decade. Overall, the school's average of all of its undergraduate and graduate rankings is #19 in the U.S. and when research is taken into account, the Smith School is among the top 15 U.S. business schools.

While in 1998 the school had no programs or departments ranked in the top 25, today there are many such rankings. For example, in 2005/06, the following areas were recognized by one or more surveys as being among the nation's best programs:

• Information Systems	Top 10
• Quantitative Analysis	Top 15
• Supply Chain/Logistics	Top 10
• Entrepreneurship	Top 15
• Management	Top 10
• Productions/Operations Management	Top 20
• Finance	Top 25
• Marketing	Top 15
• Custom Executive Programs	Top 5

The three major drivers in business are: the transformation of business driven by technology; the movement towards entrepreneurial management and partnership models in small, medium and large businesses alike; and the global character of business and competition. In each of these areas, technology plays a pivotal role. Therefore, we are differentiating the school around activities built around technology in the global economy since changes in business schools must mirror (and most desirably, lead) changes in the business environment. To emphasize this strategy, the school has adopted the branding tag line: Leaders for the Digital Economy.

FIVE YEAR OBJECTIVES

By the year 2011, The Smith School, through its portfolio of programs (research, curricula, and outreach), will be viewed as one of the best business schools in the world. It will be known for superb academic programs that integrate traditional business functions with the technological underpinnings required for leadership in the global digital economy.

The Smith School will have key programs, centers and partnerships located in significant centers around the world. These programs and partnerships will allow the ready and freely flowing exchange of ideas, students, faculty and corporate partners across international boundaries.

The resources available to the Smith School will enable the recruitment, development and retention of world-class faculty and staff, ongoing innovation and quality improvement in our programs, and a satisfying and supportive work environment for all members of the Robert H. Smith School of Business community.

The Smith School's status in research and recognition will place the school among the top business schools as measured by an average of all external recognition rankings and research metrics.

- At least four of the school's academic departments will be among the top 10 in research. Overall, the school will be among the top five in the world in research.
- The school's academic programs will average in the Top 15 in the United States when all program rankings — full-time and part-time MBA, undergraduate and PhD programs are considered.
- Student placement and salaries will be at or above those of our peer institutions.
- The School will have a dominant regional position in a broad family of programs and activities and will have national recognition in outreach programs such as executive and management development and entrepreneurship.
- The physical facilities will add to the Smith School's attraction and will continue to offer state-of-the-art technical capabilities that support the Smith School's net-centric agenda.

STRENGTHS AND BASELINE

Is this vision for 2011 achievable? We are confident that it is, and are steadfastly moving toward realizing this vision with progress in most areas within the school. The Smith School has attracted over 80 new faculty members over the last seven years from the world's premier research institutions, each selected for excellence in research, teaching, and their ability to advance the net-centric agenda of the school. Many faculty "superstars" are at the pinnacle of their profession and have been awarded endowed chairs or professorships in their respective fields. Sixty-seven percent of our full professors have endowed professorships or chairs. The caliber of doctoral students attracted to the school and their placement success at other research universities at graduation is steadily increasing and bringing the school to within reach of top 10 status for the doctoral program.

The strength of the faculty is perhaps the school's most significant strategic advantage. In the last decade, the production of published research in the consensus world's best research journals has soared. For example, Table 1 shows the year-by-year position with regard to total output in the 24 leading business journals indexed in the University of Texas (UT), Dallas, Top 100 Business Schools database. The rise of Smith School faculty research is unparalleled. From a position of #76 in the world in 1995, the Smith School placed #5 in the world in 2005.

Table 1: World Ranking of Annual Research Output in 24 Top Journals (http://citm.utdallas.edu/utdrankings/)

YEAR	2005	2004	2003	2002	2001	2000	1999	1998	1997	1996	1995
RANK	#5	#22	#10	#8	#11	#10	#23	#37	#39	#68	#76

Academic program quality has risen in parallel with our ascent to the top in research. Academic quality continually increases, attracting outstanding students and significant corporate recognition. The school's undergraduate program attracts spectacular students and external recognition for its programs has extended from the Maryland to the Mid-Atlantic and Northeastern United States. Forty-seven percent of the fall 2005 freshman class was out-of-state.

The school is the dominant supplier of part-time MBA education in the Washington-Baltimore region, offering part-time MBA tracks in Washington, D.C., Shady Grove and Baltimore, Maryland, serving approximately 1,000 students in evening and weekend programs. The Executive Masters in Business Administration (EMBA), a program launched in 2003, is now offered in College Park; Beijing and Shanghai, China; and Zurich, Switzerland with over 175 graduates in the last three years.

The quality of our undergraduate student is superb, and the innovative Smith Fellows program is creating a fabulous undergraduate experience. The Smith School entering freshman class quality in 2005 exceeded that for all other entering freshman classes at the College Park campus. Retention of freshman for last year's class, at 96 percent, was also at the top as were the school's graduation rates and student teaching ratings.

Our centers have achieved significant national recognition, attracted external funding, and important corporate partners. Celebrating its twentieth anniversary this year, the Dingman Center for Entrepreneurship is well established, and a leading partner to the technology entrepreneurs of the Washington-Baltimore region.

The Netcentric Research Laboratories: Supply Chain Management, Financial Markets, Electronic Markets, and Behavioral Labs are creating an integrated electronic teaching and research environment, with applications to e-commerce, supply chain management, financial markets, auctions, and consumer research. Identified as a special strength by the recent AACSB International accreditation review, the laboratories foster demonstration projects and research in these areas, as well as exploring the associated organizational and behavioral implications of these changes. This is the first such operation of its kind in the country, reflecting the vision of converging technology applications across the various functions of business. Our research centers such as Excellence in Service, Electronic Markets and Enterprises, Human Capital, Innovation, and Technology, Health Information and Decision Systems, and Supply Chain Management, are bringing added distinction to the school and creating partnerships among the school and the corporate and government communities.

The school is successfully engaging its large and established alumni base and corporate network, with the prospect of generous private giving and employment opportunities for students. The school was also the beneficiary of generous gifts to expand its facilities by adding a new wing in 2002 and an annex in 2007. The expanded Van Munching Hall will continue to provide the most advanced technological teaching environment among all leading business schools. Additional financial support from Mr. Robert H. Smith, the school's leading benefactor, has seeded new technology, branding and development initiatives. This funding is now supporting the

launch of a transformational undergraduate program for undergraduates—
"The Smith School Fellows Program" that formally begins in Fall 2006.

Table 2: Mission Baseline (Academic Year 2005/2006)

To ascend to one of the top global business schools as measured by the school's stature in research and teaching, and the quality and placement of its students. We will provide a superb research and teaching environment for our faculty and students as well as give our students a first class return on investment for their time and expense.

	BRP*	UTD*
Research (World):		
Overall School	7	12
Decision and Information Technologies:	3	3
Finance	9	18
Marketing	15	21
Management and Organization	8	6
Average Academic Program Ranking	19	

Graduate Salaries (Return on Investment)

Part-Time MBA	7 (Forbes)
Full-Time MBA	4 (of FT Top 25)
Undergraduate	Unknown

Faculty Salaries
Staff Salaries
Facilities and Computer Resources*** (Undergraduate Survey)
Facilities (Financial Times Executive Survey)
Placement and Career Services***

*Business Research Project (BRP), UT-Dallas (UTD)
**Salary Comparison Group: Berkeley, UCLA, Carnegie Mellon, Cornell, Ga. Tech, Illinois, Indiana, Michigan, Minnesota, NYU, UNC-Chapel Hill, Ohio State, Wharton, Texas-Austin, Washington, Wisconsin.
*** AACSB/EBI Undergraduate Student Survey of 156 Business Schools

COMPETITORS

The Smith School has numerous public and private business school peers and competitors. We compete with some schools, such as Georgetown, on the basis of reputation but have few other areas of competition with them. Some schools, such as University of Texas at Austin, Massachusetts Institute of Technology (MIT) or Carnegie Mellon, have substantial reputations as technology oriented schools. In other cases, individual departments (e.g., Finance) might compete with a specific school (e.g., Northwestern).

We believe that the key to long-term academic success as measured by academic reputation among other business schools is research prominence. The speed of the Smith School's rise (and similarly, the limited strength of the university's branding) explains much of its lack of recognition as a great academic institution.

Table 3 is a composite of three different business school research ratings, the Business Research Project, the University of Texas, Dallas, and the Financial Times research ranking). We believe that this is a representative indicator of the Smith School's primary research competitors. As is evident, the Smith School's competitors are recognized to be among the very best business schools in the United States.

Table 3: Top 25 Consensus* U.S. Business Schools Research Rankings (March 2006, See Table A6 in Appendix 3 for a the top 50 business school research rankings)

Rank	School	BRP 2001-05	FT 1/2006	UTD 2001-05	Average
1 Wharton		1	2	1	1.3
2 Harvard		3	1	3	2.3
3 Columbia		4	5	4	4.3
4 NYU		2	9.5	2	4.5
5. Chicago		12	4	6	7.3

6. UCLA	5	9.5	8	7.5
7. Northwestern	6	8	9	7.7
8. Stanford	13	3	11	9.0
9. MIT	8	15	5	9.3
10. Duke	10	8	12	10.0
11. UNC	9	12	16	12.3
12. Smith	**7**	**19**	**12**	**13.0**
13. So. Cal.	20	15	14	16.3
14. Texas	19	23.5	7	16.5

*Average US rank across the three major B-School research rankings (Business Research Project, Financial Times and University of Texas, Dallas)

In many areas, the school's strengths are much greater than its public recognition. For example, the Marketing Department is placed in the top 13 by Business Week On Line but otherwise appears rarely in top marketing department rankings. We have a superb Finance Department that we judge to be in the top 12 in the country based on the quality of the department's faculty, research and participation in professional activities. Public school competitors include University of California, Berkeley and University of California, Los Angeles (UCLA), while private competitors are Carnegie Mellon, Massachusetts Institute of Technology (MIT) and Stanford University. We are very well regarded among major finance departments and finance faculty, as demonstrated by our success in faculty recruiting, but the Finance Department does not get the recognition it deserves in trade magazine rankings.

Trade magazine rankings are summarized in Appendix 3. In that Appendix, Table A5 summarizes the Smith School's overall rankings in the major rankings in which we participate. The average of the Smith School rankings of its degree programs is #19 and when this is averaged with its #12 research average, the school has reached its target to be a Top 15 business school.

For the purposes of accreditation by AACSB International, the Smith School's current peers and aspirant group are given in Table 4.

Table 4: AACSB Int. Comparable Peers and Aspirant Group Smith Brand Recognition – 19, Research Rank – 12, Overall – 15. Comparable Peers – Average brand recognition, research rank, overall average

University of Texas at Austin – 16, 14, **17**	University of Michigan – 3, 26, **16**
University of Indiana – 22, 20, **20**	University of CA – Berkeley – 4, 18, **9**

Ohio State University – 29, 19, 22   Michigan State University – 34, 15, 21

Aspirant Group – Average brand recognition, research rank, overall average

Harvard University – 5, 2, **2**	New York University – 8, 4, **5**
University of Chicago – 2, 5, **3**	Stanford – 20, 8, **11**
MIT – 12, 9, **10**	Columbia University –6, 3, **4**

FINANCIAL STRATEGY

While the Smith School is a public business school within the flagship public university of the State of Maryland, the financial position of the school more closely resembles a private institution. About 10 percent of the school's support is from the State of Maryland. The school, like many other major public business schools does not retain its undergraduate tuition nor the university specified graduate tuition for its full-time MBA students. In return, the school receives a "base budget." In the Smith School's case, the university retains $19-20 million in tuition revenues and provides a "base budget" of about $16 million in return. In addition, the school receives university services such as university paid employee fringe benefits (social security, employee retirement, and health insurance), some facilities maintenance and personnel, financial and developmental services.

The school generates additional revenues with activities such as its Executive MBA Program (EMBA), non-degree executive education and its part-time MBA programs. Various agreements with the university define revenue sharing and tax structures for each program. Total Smith School revenues have grown from approximately $15 million in 1998 to $56 million in the academic year ending June 2006.

The school uses a five-year forecasting model to report and project revenues by category, product line and location. This model augments an operational budget reporting system that interfaces with the university's accounting systems. The forecasting system enables the Smith School to investigate various tuition/cost scenarios as well as to incorporate hiring, operational and facilities investments. Figure 1 shows the historical distribution of the school's revenues as well as the forecast for academic year (AY) 2005/06, 2007 and 2008. The portion marked "University Paid Benefits" is a crude estimate of the value of the employee benefits and other services paid by the university on behalf of the Smith School.

Private contributions are a very important part of the school's financial plan. However, significant revenue growth is also required for the school to meet its ambitious goals. The Smith School plans to add 20-3 0 faculty members in the next three years. The school seeks to double its marketing and communications budget over the next five years and must increase its information technology support, and alumni and development activities by 35 percent each. Another significant challenge is to grow funding for the Smith Undergraduate Fellows program from a very small base to well over $1.5 million per year.

Figure 1: Robert H. Smith Actual and Projected Revenues
(1998-2006 actual, 2007 budget, 2008 projected)

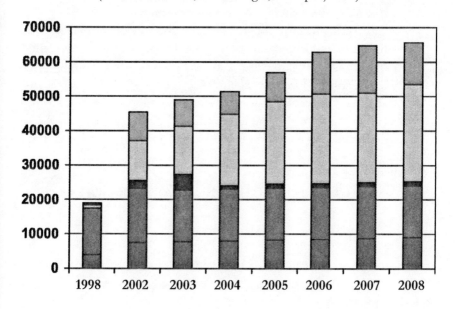

STRATEGIC PRIORITIES

The school has attracted world-class faculty, enhanced the distinctiveness and caliber of its programs and centers, and improved the financial and administrative elements of its infrastructure. It has also achieved recognition nationally and internationally for several competencies such as the technology focus of the school and our activities in entrepreneurship. However, we have not yet reached the status to which we aspire.

In our continued campaign toward attaining our strategic goals and correcting areas of weakness, we continue our focus on several strategic priorities:

- Transforming research excellence to research greatness throughout the school while better integrating appreciation for advanced business research in our academic programs.
- Transforming academic programs from excellent to great.

- Building the Smith community to create a dynamic faculty, staff, student, and alumni network.
- Extending the school's advantage in information technology as a core competency throughout the school, in all of the school's functions and among staff, departments, and academic programs.
- Marketing the distinctions of the school with special emphasis on the school's global activities, leading edge strategic analysis and application of technology and entrepreneurship leadership.
- Increasing resources and infrastructure support for the school. The next section outlines, the tactics underlying each of these strategic priorities.

TACTICS FOR ACADEMIC YEARS 2006 - 2011

Research Greatness

Transform research excellence to research greatness throughout the school while better integrating appreciation for advanced business research in our academic programs.

- Continue to recruit internationally recognized faculty stars and continue "signature" hires of senior faculty with major international reputations and leading research records throughout the school.
- Continue to build department research reputations by promoting existing capabilities and accomplishments.
- Exploit and improve synergies across departments in joint leading edge research and department capabilities.
- Continue bringing to Smith high-visibility research seminars and national conferences with the goal of one major event per month.
- Continue to strengthen mentor and support systems for junior faculty in each area to position them for promotion and tenure.
- Support and increase faculty research grant activities and develop additional summer research funding opportunities for tenured faculty.
- Continue to increase funding and reduce workload for PhD students to support top talent. Increase placement opportunities

for Ph.D. students with earlier and more stringent research paper requirements.

- Expand the Smith Undergraduate Research Fellow Program and provide research fellowships for undergraduate students to assist faculty in faculty research.
- Provide to star potential PhD students, fifth year fellowships and post doctoral support.

Academic Program Distinctions

Transform Smith academic programs from excellent to great.

- Design and implement the Smith Undergraduate Fellows Program. Introduce the Smith Freshman/Sophomore Fellows Program in AY 2006/07 and the Smith Junior/Senior Fellows Program in AY2007/08. Roll out Junior/Senior Fellows tracks in 2007 and 2008 so that all students have the opportunity to participate in at least one Fellows track.
- Define, design and implement a transformational MBA program (both core and electives) that elevates the MBA experience from excellent to great. Complete the initial design and begin implementation in 2006/2007. Find mechanisms to integrate the Smith brand into the curriculum.
- Continue enhancing the part-time MBA program with additional student services, teaching quality improvements, technology advances and physical infrastructure improvements.
- Continue expansion of our activities in China.
- Explore the development of specialized EMBA and Master of Science programs such as supply chain management, technology management and health information and decision systems programs/concentration. Develop opportunities for combined 5-year undergraduate and MS programs. This step will require establishing appropriate revenue sharing arrangements with the university.
- Fully develop our partnerships in Europe and offer intercontinental opportunities in Asia, Europe and the United States for EMBA and MBA students. Develop a joint degree program in India and

identify additional operating location targets to extend the school's global presence.

- Create an accelerated global part-time MBA program that utilizes the resources and relationships of our international partners.
- Identify future locations in Latin and South America for the global expansion of the school.
- Maintain high teaching quality across all levels of the undergraduate programs and all locations of the MBA program. Improve teaching support for faculty and begin the development of a series of expanded teaching quality enhancements.
- Strengthen the focus of faculty efforts for the PhD program towards placement of students in the very top business schools and develop departmental incentive systems that encourage top placements.

Building the Smith Community

Build the Smith community to create a dynamic faculty, staff, student, and alumni network.

- Continue building the Smith community of students, faculty, alumni and recruiters—integrating activities of student, alumni and mentoring programs with special effort on building the part-time/full-time MBA student/alumni network
- Improve the school's governance system, accountability and reporting systems, and committee and organizational structures to stimulate the development of the Smith community, marketing efforts, program delivery and operational efficiencies in line with the Smith School's emergence as a mature top research institution.
- Refine faculty service standards and metrics to reflect the importance of faculty collaboration in building a strong Smith community culture.
- Execute coordinated strategies to build and strengthen corporate partnerships that will lead to increased student career opportunities, research, sponsorship and philanthropic support of key Smith School initiatives.
- Review the mentoring program, evaluate the effectiveness of the program and revise to improve operations and student/alumni

satisfaction. Extend the mentoring program to undergraduate students by 2008.

- Integrate center, academic and external relations event programming and sponsorship into a unified strategy for corporate sponsorship and fund raising.
- Begin the development of an Alumni Development Program.

IT as a Core Competency

Extend the school's advantage in information technology as a core competency throughout the school, in all of the school's functions and among staff, departments and academic programs, system implementations and programs.

- Continue to extend the ability of the school to offer advanced technological capabilities everywhere the school operates around the world and insure that potential users are aware of these capabilities and trained for their use.
- Revise and centralize the management of the Smith Information Technology Integration Program to better support teaching and research within the departments and centers.
- Expand the portfolio of executive and management education programs to focus on technology content, clientele, and advanced learning tools.
- Enhance technology integration of courses with finance, supply chain, behavior, and electronic markets laboratories.
- Selectively develop new courses, simulations and applications that utilize technology in accounting systems, electronic market mechanisms, finance trading floor and simulations, and hi-tech marketing and management.
- Enhance the use of technology in course delivery, including better training of faculty and students in accessing, storing, communicating and processing digital course material.
- Expand student involvement in the Netcentric Laboratories and extend key elements of the laboratories to part-time locations.
- Sustain and expand collaborative, inter-disciplinary research within departments, across the Smith School and across colleges.

Marketing the School

Market the distinctions of the school with special emphasis on the school's global activities, leading edge application of technology and entrepreneurship.

- Expand the school's branding activities through increased promotion and advertising using traditional, video and web-based media and also expand departmental functional branding efforts.
- Enhance the global branding of the Smith School with special activities in China, India, Europe, the Middle East and South America.
- Continue to develop branding materials that help students, alumni and recruiters translate the Smith School strategy into clearly understood career benefits.
- Support the school's research centers to advance faculty expertise while serving as a focal point for external recognition and business partnerships.
- Expand advisory board activities to advance business partnerships, research opportunities, financial support, and student placement
- Maintain the number of high-visibility research symposia with at least one major symposium per department per year and overall, hold at least one significant public symposium, conference or event at the Smith School each month during the academic year.
- Achieve placement goals for PhD students in top 50 business schools and research universities.

Resources and Infrastructure

Increase resources and infrastructure support for the school.

- Plan, design and construct the annex to Van Munching Hall with targeted occupancy in AY 2007/08.
- Continue to automate the back office operations of the business school as an element of the school's major IT initiatives.
- Continue improving operational processes within administrative and program offices.

- Provide the best possible work climate for all staff including professional skills development for all levels of staff.
- Continue the silent phase of the development campaign to be completed by FY20 12 to secure major commitments from alumni, friends and corporations in the $75-100 million range.
- Continue revenue generating entrepreneurial activities aimed at sustaining Smith School revenue growth at a pace sufficient to continue expansion of faculty to 150 by 2009, maintain salaries at the median of the top 10 business schools, maintain our technological lead, build the Smith brand and fuel our global expansion.
- Develop and launch a series of revenue-generating, high-value Master of Science degree programs to our undergraduate students and new students in Maryland and abroad.
- Increase overall revenues for the school so that by 2011, the school has total revenues among the top three public business schools.

Appendix 1

ADMINISTRATIVE AND FINANCIAL

Figure A1: Robert H. Smith School of Business Organizational Structure

Dean

Senior Associate Dean

Manager, Academic Scheduling

Centers	Academic Departments	Smith School Support	Educational Programs
	Information Technology		

Dingman Center for Entrepreneurship

Excellence in Service

Electronic Markets and Enterprises

Global Business

Health Information and Decision Systems

Human Capital, Technology & Innovation

Supply Chain

Managerment

Accounting and Information Assurance

Decision & Information Technology

Director, Technology Resources

Infrastructure Support   Academic Applications

QUEST

Finance

Logistics, Business & Public Policy

Management & Organization

Marketing

Figure A2: Strategic Planning Process

The Smith School operates a continuous improvement model spearheaded by its strategic planning process. This process began in the 1997/98 academic year. Under this model, annual and five-year objectives and tactics are set in six areas: research, academic programs, the Smith community, information technology, marketing, and resources and infrastructure.

Each department (academic and administrative) participates in the strategic plan, sets strategic objectives for itself as well as collaborating in the statement of objectives for the school. The school's department chairs and senior staff (assistant, associate deans and department directors) led by the Dean's Office, insure the implementation of the objectives.

The strategic planning process operates on the following time-table.

- June - Finalize Faculty Recruiting Plan
- September - Satisfaction Surveys Completed for Baseline
  - ☐ Faculty Satisfaction
  - ☐ Undergraduate Student Satisfaction
  - ☐ MBA Student Satisfaction
  - ☐ External Rankings
- November – Management Strategy Retreat
- February – Department Strategic Plans and research metrics
- March – April Integration of strategies, plans, and financial forecasts
- May – Strategic Plan Presented at School Assembly and to MBA Students
- May – Draft Plan Published for Review and Feedback
- April – May Strategic PRD Objectives for next year
- June – Plan Published

August - Planning Cycle Begins Again

Goals and Objectives	Baseline Data	Management Retreat	Department Plan Reviews	Plan Presentation	**Publish Plan**

Table A1. Smith School Pro Forma Financial Forecast ($000)

Revenues	2004	2005	2006	2007	2008	2008
Hard Budget	13,764	14,769	15,834	15,959	15,959	15,959
Other Univ.	776	1,403	1,953	1,855	2,435	3,035
Tuition/ Fees	20,732	23,923	25,904	28,917	31,340	33,022
Private	6,568	8,787	12,993	18,277	13,804	12,228
Total Revenues	41,840	48,882	56,684	64,112	63,557	64,264
Prior Year Fore		6,260	53,399	60,206	54,494	56,222

Note: Private Revenues include contributions and payouts for Annex: 2006: $1,230 K: 2007: $7,000 K; 2008: $2,945 K.

Table A2. Smith School Key Expenditure Forecast

Faculty Hires	1,610	1,916
Retention/Raises	888	1,165
Summer Research Fund	450	450
Career Services	1.767	1,867
Strategic Marketing	1,818	2,318
Ph.D. Student Support	1414	1489
MBA Student Support	1,400	1,400
Smith Fellows Program	231	531
Alumni/Development	1,135	1,335
IT Technology/Labs	2,572	3,050
IT Capital Improvements	450	0
Facilities Improvements/Annex	1,960	7,260

Appendix 2

ACADEMIC PROGRAMS

Table A3: Program Sizes for Top 25 Schools in 2006 *Financial Times* MBA Rankings

		Undergrads	FT MBA	PT MBA	EMBA	PhD
1	University of Pennsylvania:	2,466	1,615	2466	402	184
2	Harvard Business School	0	1,823	0	0	31
3	Stanford University GSB	0	749	0	0	101
4	Columbia Business School	0	1,180	0	618	103
5	University of Chicago GSB	0	1,093	1481	516	114
6	New York University: Stern	2,328	776	1180	173	100
7	Dartmouth College: Tuck	0	504	0	0	0
8	MIT: Sloan	400	710	0	0	80
9	Yale School of Management	0	?	?	?	?
10	University of Michigan: Ross	717	891	847	115	84
11	UC Berkeley: Haas	700	489	694	129	82
12	Northwestern University: Kellogg	0	1,310	1150	400	124
13	UCLA: Anderson	0	660	600	140	64
14	University of Virginia: Darden	0	625	0	0	10
15	Duke University: Fuqua	0	831	60	600	82
16	University of North Carolina:	705	558	0	317	57
17	Michigan State University: Broad	4,681	195	219	103	82
18	University of Iowa: Tippie	1,122	122	680	163	102
19	Cornell University: Johnson	0	581	0	110	38
19	Georgetown University:	1,304	501	60	102	0
21	University of Maryland: Smith	2,881	262	1014	129	106
22	University of Illinois, Urbana-	3,021	191	0	54	87
23	University of Rochester: Simon	0	244	158	137	63
24	Carnegie Mellon: Tepper	575	316	163	0	102
25	Emory University: Goizueta	552	346	197	130	37
25	Pennsylvania State: Smeal	4,791	139	0	45	68

NOTES: 10 of the top 15 programs have no undergraduate programs. Yale does not publish the size of their program. Virginia has a separate Undergraduate School of Business. Georgetown and Dartmouth have no PhD programs

Table A4: Academic Programs at Smith:

2005 Graduates with Bachelor of Science Degree programs with majors in:	878*
Accounting	134
Information Systems	53
Finance	242
General Business and Management	53
Human Resources Management	3
International Business	93
Logistics and Transportation	83
Marketing	209
Operations and Quality Management	8
2005 MBA Graduates	**452**
MS Degree Programs	**6**
Ph.D. Program	**17**

* Sum of individual undergraduates in majors may not equal total number of graduates because of graduates with dual majors.

- Approximately 2,800 undergraduates ranging from freshman to seniors majoring in business at College Park and Shady Grove, Md.
- 255 full-time MBA students in College Park, Md., from 32 countries.
- 1,000 part-time MBA students attending weekend and evening programs in Washington, D.C., Shady Grove, and Baltimore, Md.
- 170 Executive MBA participants in the U.S. and China
- 105 PhD students from 22 countries (Approximate figures, fall 2005)

Table A5a: Average Student Evaluations- Course Level

Evaluation Results by Course Level

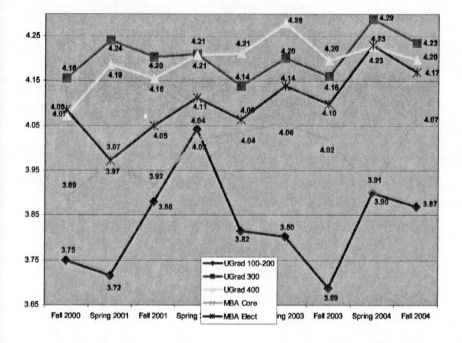

Table A5b: Average Student Evaluations- Spring, Fall 2005
(5.0 maximum)

DEPART-MENT	Spring 2005		Fall 2005	
	# OF SECTIONS	AVERAGE	# OF SECTIONS	AVERAGE
ACCT	42	4.19	42	4.25
DIT	51	4.19	48	4.16
FIN	53	4.04	55	4.25
LBPP	54	4.34	48	4.25
MKTG	61	4.27	44	4.19
M&O	50	4.24	41	4.34
OCM (BMGT 367)	4	4.11	6	4.15
SMITH	314	4.16	284	4.24
Area				
CP UG Lower	10	3.69	15	4.11
CP UG Upper	152	4.13	131	4.31
Shady Grove UG	19	4.41	24	4.38
CP MBA	63	4.24	49	4.20
DC MBA	52	4.12	41	4.06
Shady Grove MBA	8	4.15	12	4.12
Baltimore	10	4.03	12	4.16

Appendix 3

RANKINGS

Table A6: Average Program and Research Rankings

MBA Avg.	UG	PT MBA	PhD	Average Overall Program Rank	Research Rank	
3.0	1.0		1	1	1	1. Wharton
5.8			8	5	2	2. Harvard
5.5		2.5	7	2	5	3. Chicago
6.3			9	6	3	4. Columbia
11.0	7.0	1.0	22	8	4	5. NYU
14.3		3.0	15	9	6	6. UCLA
15.5	7.0		16	10	11	7. UNC
5.3		3.5	43	13	7	8. Northwestern
10.8	3.5	7.2	4	4	18	9. UC Berkeley
10.0	2.0		39	12	9	10. MIT
5.5			33	20	8	11. Stanford
14.8	-		20	14	10	12. Duke
15.0	7.0	8.0	3	7	21	13. Carnegie
24.7	9.5	5.0	28	11	13	14. So. Cal.
29.2	**24.0**	**10.0**	**13**	**19**	**12**	**15. R. H. Smith**
10.2	6.0	6.0	2	3	26	16. Michigan
35.3	14.5	7.5	18	17	17	18. Minnesota
27.5	7.0	45.0	14	15	14	17. Texas
21.2	19.5	15.5	46	30	16	19. Emory
24.0	11.0		30	22	20	20. Indiana
26.7	24.0	30.0	30	34	15	21. Michigan St.
30.1	19.5	26.0	26	29	19	22. Ohio State
27.8	14.5	11.0	40	23	22	23. Wash. U.
37.1	14.5		5	18	27	24. Illinois

33.4	19.5		27	31	23	25. Penn State
41.9	14.5		24	33	24	26. Wisconsin
37.5	24.0		12	28	28	27. Washington
29.0	14.5		29	26	29	28. Purdue
5.0			44	27	30	29. Dartmouth
45.5	28.	12.5	10	24	31	30. Arizona St.
13.5	14.		36	21	34	31. Cornell
48.4	28			1	35	25	32. Florida
11.3				3	25	35	33. Yale
11.3	9.5			3	16	45	34. Virginia
46.5	19.5				37	33	35. Arizona
33.5	24			5	42	32	36. Notre Dame
29.8		3	3	36	37		37. Rochester
41.6	32.0	1	4	39	41		38. Boston Coll.
38.3	37.0	1	5	41	44		39. SMU
42.3	32.0		6	32	53		40. Georgia
32.5	28.0	3	4	40	46		41 Georgetown
29.4	37.0	3	3	38	49		42. Iowa
42.7	32.0		2	43	45		44. Texas A&M
61.1	32.0		2	44	44		43. Case Western
28.5	43.5		4	45	57		45. BYU
37.1	32.0		5	46	59		46. Wake Forest
34.3	50.0		4	47	65		47. Vanderbilt
37.9	50.0		4	48	63		48. Wm. & Mary
47.5	50.0		4	49	61		49. Thunderbird
48.0	50.0		5	50	66		50. UC Davis

Table A7: Consensus* Top 50 US Business Schools
Research Rankings (March 2006)

School	25-Feb 2006 BRP	6-Jan 2006 FT	25-Feb 2006 UTD	AVERAGE
1. Wharton	1	2	1	1.3
2. Harvard	3	1	3	2.3
3. Columbia	4	5	4	4.3
4. NYU	2	9.5	2	4.5
5. Chicago	12	4	6	7.3
6. UCLA	5	9.5	8	7.5
7. Northwestern	6	8	9	7.7
8. Stanford	13	3	11	9.0
9. MIT	8	15	5	9.3
10. Duke	10	8	12	10.0
11. UNC	9	12	16	12.3
12. Smith	**7**	**19**	**12**	**13.0**
13. So. Cal.	20	15	14	16.3
14. Texas	19	23.5	7	16.5
15. Mich. St.	11	23.5	18	17.5
16. Emory	23	15	19	19.0
17. Minnesota	16	19	25	20.0
18. UC Berkeley	25	6	30	20.3
17. Ohio State	18	23.5	21	20.8
20. Indiana	17	--	25	21.0
21. Carnegie	27	17	23	22.3
22. Wash. U.	32	12	24	22.7
23. Penn State	24	28	17	23.0
24. Wisconsin	15	31.5	26	24.2
25. Florida	14	23.5	37	24.8

26. Michigan	58	7	10	25.0
27. Illinois	21	35	22	26.0
28. U. Wash.	31	28	20	26.3
29. Purdue	22	33.5	27	27.5
30. Dartmouth	40	12	34	28.7
31. Arizona St.	29	31.5	29	29.8
32. Notre Dame	30	28	34	30.7
33. Arizona	50	--	48	32.7
34. Cornell	44	23.5	31	32.8
35. Yale	39	23.5	36	32.8
36. UC Irvine	48	19	32	33.0
37. Rochester	28	36	35	33.0
38. Tulane	59	--	47	35.3
39. Pitt	35	--	41	38.0
40. So. Carolina	33	--	43	38.0
41. BC	36	38	42	38.7
42. Utah	40	--	38	39.0
43. UT Dallas	45	--	33	39.0
44. Case Western	43	33.5	44	40.2
45. Texas A&M	57	32.5	39	42.8
46. Boston U.	54	35	40	43.0
47. Connecticut	41	--	45	43.0
48. Colorado	36	--	53	44.5
49. Georgia St.	44	--	46	45.0
50. Georgetown	51	45	49	48.3

*Average U.S. rank across the three major B-School research rankings: Business Research Project, University of Texan, Dallas, and Financial Times.

Table A8: Summary of Smith School External Rankings, AY 2001-2006

School-wide

#15   Regional School (WSJ)
#3   Hidden Gem (WSJ, 2002)
#6, 8   Public B-Schools (FT, BW)
#7   Research – (Businesresearch.ca: 2001-2005)
#7   Part-Time MBA Program (Forbes)
#13   Part-Time MBA Program (USN)
#8   Teaching- (BW-2003)
#22   UG Program (USN)
#21   Intellectual Capital (BW)
#21   MBA Program in US (FT-2005)
#28   MBA Program (BW)
#29   Full Time MBA Program (Forbes)
#3,   Top 25 Techno-MBA (Computerworld)
Top 20 Tech-Savvy B-schools (Tech 2.0)
Top 13 Entrepreneurship (Entrepreneur Magazine)

Students and Alumni

#1-4   Value for the Money among Top 25 US schools (FT 2001-2006)
#1   Entrepreneurship (Alumni- Entrepreneurship Magazine, 2004)
#1   Among Management Consulting Recruiters (WSJ, 2004)
#5   Among Technology Recruiters (World) (WSJ)
#7   Graduate Satisfaction (FT, 2003)
#7   Communications-Interpersonal Skills (WSJ, 2002)
#8   Ability to Work in Teams (WSJ, 2002)
#15   Student Satisfaction (BW-2003)
#11   Placement rate in of Top 25 US Schools (FT)
#13   Salary Alumni Salary Increase of Top 25 U.S. Schools (FT, 2005)
#10   Alumni Aims Achieved (US) (FT)

Academic Programs

#4	E-Commerce (USN, 2004)
#7	Information Technology (WSJ)
#5,7	IS (USN)
#7	Financial Services (WSJ, 2002)
#8,12	Supply Chain Management (USN) Top 13, Marketing (BW Online)
#13,17	Entrepreneurship (USN)
#18	Marketing (USN)
#22	Finance (USN)
#9, 21	Management (USN)
#13	Doctoral Program Rank, US, (FT)
#24	Production/Operations Management (USN)
#5	(US),
#8	(World) Customized Executive Education, US, (Economist)
#14	(US),
#22	(World) Customized Executive Education, World, (FT)
"A"	Curriculum, Ethics (BW-2003)

Appendix 4

RESEARCH

Table A9: Smith School Consensus Top Business Journals by Area

Accounting & Information Assurance
- The Accounting Review
- The Journal of Accounting Research
- The Journal of Accounting and Economics
- Journal of Accounting and Public Policy

Information Systems
- Information Systems Research
- Management Science
- Management Information Systems Quarterly

Management Science/Operations Research
- Management Science
- INFORMS Journal on Computing
- Operations Research
- Transportation Science

Operations Management
- Management Science
- Manufacturing & Service Operations Management
- Operations Research
- Production and Operations Management

Business Statistics
- Journal of the American Statistical Association
- Journal of the Royal Statistical Society
- Technometrics
- Journal of Computational and Graphical Statistics
- Journal of Business and Economic Statistics

Finance
- Journal of Finance

- Journal of Financial Economics
- Review of Financial Studies
- American Economic Review
- Journal of Economic Theory
- Rand Journal
- Journal of Business

Business Law
- The American Business Law Journal
- Law journals published by the top law schools

International Business
- The Journal of International Business Studies
- Also top economic journals and top management journals

Logistics and Transportation
- Transportation Research
- The Journal of Business Logistics
- The Transportation Journal
- Transportation Science

Management & Organization
- Administrative Science Quarterly
- Academy of Management Journal
- Academy of Management Review
- Strategic Management Journal
- Management Science
- Organization Science
- Journal of Applied Psychology
- Organizational Behavior and Human Decision Processes
- Journal of Personality and Social Psychology

Marketing
- Journal of Marketing
- Journal of Marketing Research
- Marketing Science
- Journal of Consumer Research

Table A10: Top Research Competitors
Source: Business Research Project, 2001-2005

Top 15 Research Schools (World)
University of Pennsylvania, The Wharton School
New York University, Stern School of Business
Harvard University, Harvard Business School
Columbia University, Graduate School of Business
University of California - Los Angeles, Anderson Graduate School of Management Northwestern University, Kellogg Graduate School of Management
University of Maryland, Robert H. Smith School Business
Massachusetts Institute of Technology, Sloan School of Management
University of North Carolina, Kenan-Flagler School of Business
Duke University, Fuqua School of Business
Michigan State University, The Eli Broad College of Business
University of Chicago Graduate School of Business
INSEAD
Stanford University, Graduate School of Business
University of Florida, Warrington College of Business

Top 15 U.S. Finance Departments
New York University, Stern School of Business
University of Pennsylvania, The Wharton School
University of California - Los Angeles, Anderson Graduate School of Management Harvard University, Harvard Business School
University of Chicago, Graduate School of Business
Massachusetts Institute of Technology, Sloan School of Management
Emory University, Goizueta Business School
Columbia University, Graduate School of Business
University of Maryland, Robert H. Smith School Business University of Notre Dame, Mendoza College of Business
The Pennsylvania State University, Smeal College of Business Duke University, Fuqua School of Business
University of Rochester, Simon School of Business Administration Northwestern University, Kellogg Graduate School of Management Indiana University, Kelley School of Business

Top 15 U.S. Marketing Departments

Northwestern University, Kellogg Graduate School of Management

University of Pennsylvania, The Wharton School

Columbia University, Graduate School of Business

Duke University, Fuqua School of Business

University of Florida, Warrington College of Business

University of California - Berkeley, Haas School of Business Administration

University of California - Los Angeles, Anderson Graduate School of Management University of Southern California, Marshall School of Business

University of Chicago, Graduate School of Business

University of Wisconsin, School of Business Administration

Dartmouth College, Tuck School of Business Administration

New York University, Stern School of Business

Harvard University, Harvard Business School

The Pennsylvania State University, Smeal College of Business

University of Maryland, Robert H. Smith School Business

Top 15 U.S. Decision and Information Technologies Departments (Information Systems, Operations and Production)

University of Pennsylvania, The Wharton School

Columbia University, Graduate School of Business

University of Maryland, Robert H. Smith School Business

Michigan State University, The Eli Broad College of Business

University of California - Los Angeles, Anderson Graduate School of Management University of Minnesota, Carlson School of Business

Massachusetts Institute of Technology, Sloan School of Management

University of Texas, Austin, College of Business Administration

Stanford University, Graduate School of Business

Carnegie Mellon University, Tepper School of Business

University of North Carolina, Kenan-Flagler School of Business

Duke University, Fuqua School of Business

Harvard University, Harvard Business School

University of Texas- Dallas, The School of Management

New York University, Stern School of Business

Top 15 U.S. Management and Organization Departments (Strategy, Organization and Human Resources)

University of Pennsylvania, The Wharton School

University of Florida, Warrington College of Business Michigan State University, The Eli Broad College of Business Harvard University, Harvard Business School

University of Wisconsin, School of Business Administration Purdue University, Krannert School of Management

The Ohio State University, Fisher College of Business University of Maryland, Robert H. Smith School Business University of North Carolina, Kenan-Flagler School of Business Indiana University, Kelley School of Business

Emory University, Goizueta Business School

Northwestern University, Kellogg School of Management New York University, Stern School of Business

Columbia University, Columbia Business School University of Minnesota, Carlson School of Business

Top 15 U.S. International Business and Entrepreneurship

Rensselaer Polytechnic Institute, Lally School of Management and Technology University of Pennsylvania, The Wharton School Ohio State University, Fisher College of Business Case Western Reserve, Weatherhead School of Management Harvard University, Harvard Business School

University of South Carolina, Darla Moore School of Business

University of Maryland, Robert H. Smith School of Business

University of Colorado, Graduate Business School

University of Illinois, College of Commerce and Business Administration

Massachusetts Institute of Technology, Sloan School of Management

University of California, Los Angeles, Anderson Graduate School of Management Columbia University, Graduate School of Business University of Miami, School of Business Administration Indiana University, Kelley School of Business New York University, Stern School of Business

Appendix 5

THE SMITH SCHOOL UNDERGRADUATE
FELLOWS PROGRAM

In his September 13, 2004 address to the University, "Taking Stock: State of the University," President Mote stated:

> "I strongly believe that every student should have the opportunity for a special program experience. We're not quite there yet, but we'll be there soon. I am very grateful to the provost and his staff for creating a new program that they call the President's Promise. The President's Promise will guarantee a special program opportunity for all students entering as freshmen in Fall 2005. The programs will include study abroad, internships in government and the private sector, research and independent study and so on. When fully implemented, this Promise will complete our pledge.

> My personal view is that international experience should be a high priority for all our students. In 2004 one cannot be fully educated without an understanding of the values and circumstances of other cultures that can only be acquired through first hand experience. There is no replacing being there."

Competition for the best and brightest students among top-ranked business schools is extremely high. The Robert H. Smith School undergraduate program has achieved excellence will expand its range of distinctive and quality programs to move from excellence to greatness. Special programs currently offered by the Smith School, such as Quest and Business Honors, reach only some of the highly talented students entering each year. Hence the primary goal of the Smith School Fellows Program is to offer a set of special opportunities to all of our directly admitted freshmen and sophomores and at a later date to offer all students, (direct admits as well as internal and external transfer students), special program options in their Junior and Senior years.

The Smith Fellows program begins in the freshman year with the Smith Freshman/Sophomore Fellows Program for all directly admitted freshmen (approximately 400 per year). These students will participate as a cohort in a broad range of academic and co-curricular activities to enrich their education, and create a strong bond of community among the members of the class.

The Freshman Fellows will be introduced early in their academic careers to the distinctive features of Smith School's approach to business education and research. Experiential components of the initiative will range from single events to year-long projects (examples include film series and field trips that highlight faculty-student shared experiences.) A number of students will be given the opportunity to gain international experience in keeping with President Mote's objectives.

As part of the Freshman/Sophomore Fellows Program, the Smith School redesigned its academic program, expanded undergraduate advising, and developed a group of co-curricular activities such as summer orientation, film series, field trips, monthly socials, an emerging leaders retreat, service projects, special career training and events and international study trips. The introductory BMGT 110 course was revamped and now includes two new core topics: business ethics and the impact of technology on business practices. In this way, the Smith School will place additional emphasis on two themes in which it continues to pursue a leadership role. The course has also been taken from a large 250-student lecture format to eight classes each with 40-50 students. Freshman and sophomore seminars have been added and the junior level career preparation course has been moved to the sophomore year. During the sophomore year, the Smith Fellows will be introduced to the Junior/Senior Fellows Programs with the goal that all students will have the opportunity to participate in one or more special opportunities for which they are qualified.

The Junior/Senior Fellows Program

All students will have the option to participate in at least one special experience. To achieve this goal, existing programs are being expanded or modified and new programs and initiatives are being launched. These include:

1.   **Expanding the Smith School Honors Program**

The Smith School Honors Program, which currently includes approximately 30 students per year, will be expanded into two tracks of 30 students each in 2007. This will require adding 3-6 junior and senior year honors courses. The program includes (starting in Winter 2005) a 3-credit international study trip. This course will be repeated annually and expanded in line with the expansion of the Honors Program.

2.   **QUEST**

The Quality Enhancement Systems and Teams Program (QUEST), co-managed by the Robert H. Smith School of Business and the A. James Clark School of Engineering, currently serves approximately 80 students/year, primarily divided between business and engineering but also serving a few CMPS students. About 35 Smith students participate each year. This program will be maintained at its current size but expanded if the School of Engineering is able to support its portion of the cost of expansion.

3.   **Smith Technology Scholars Program**

We currently have an initiative underway that includes 10-15 undergraduate students and dedicated technical staff. The initiative is expanding faculty technology support for teaching and research through the use of technology specialists and undergraduate student "technology" assistants serving on a paid basis.

4.   **Smith Faculty Research Fellows Initiative**

We began the Research Fellows Program in 2005/06 to provide faculty with paid undergraduate research assistants. The program began with 22 students in AY 2006. It will be expanded to 30 students in 2006 and 40 students in 2007. In its first year, the program has been exceptionally well received by both students and faculty.

5.   General Business Entrepreneurship Fellows

The Smith School Faculty revised its undergraduate General Business Major to include a four-course undergraduate entrepreneurship track. Entrepreneurship students will work with our Dingman Center for Entrepreneurship in business plan competitions, business development projects and many other activities. Undergraduate entrepreneurship courses are already being offered and the Entrepreneurship Fellows Track formally begins in our Shady Grove program in Fall 2006. We expect that this program would appeal to approximately 50-100 students per year. To support this option, the Smith School is hiring additional entrepreneurship faculty.

6.   The Smith Six Sigma Fellows Program

The Smith School has already designed and delivered courses in Six Sigma for its undergraduate students as part of both QUEST and the operations management curriculum. Under this initiative, these offerings will, be transformed into a structured sequence of two courses and an associated business project. Armed with the fundamentals and practical skills of the Six Sigma approach, students will graduate with credentials that are valued by today's leading business enterprises.

7.   The Smith International Fellows Program

The Smith School is currently recruiting for a fall 2006 class of 20-40 students with dual majors in business and language. These students will receive special multicultural business training as well as participate in subsidized international study trips.

8.   Global Opportunities

The Global Opportunities Program will replace the discontinued Business, Culture and Languages program operated by the College of Arts and Humanities (ARHU). Under the expired program, languages students were allowed to take a few available courses in the business school and business students interested in languages took electives or occasionally double majored in languages. The new program will be jointly managed by the

Smith School and ARHU. Student selection procedures are being refined and individual business school advising for business courses will be provided for all students so that student needs are best matched with available business courses. International (possibly school funded) study trips for business students will be developed.

9.   Smith Talent Acquisition and Referral System (STARS)

The goals of STARS is to attract low income and minority students to the study of business; to support and mentor high school students to meet Smith School undergraduate admissions standards; and to support and mentor students through college to meet graduation requirements. STARS was launched in the 2002-2003 academic year and currently sponsors activities such as: The STARS Retreat, Academic Success Field Day, High School to College Admissions Days, ESOL Admissions Days (in Spanish), the Finance Field Day, and the Maryland Day Open House. The STARS program involves an array of Smith School students serving as mentors as well as Smith School staff, faculty and alumni. We will continue expanding this program and add staff resources to support and coordinate student mentoring.

10. Focused Department and Center Activities

The Smith School supports six academic departments as well as a number of centers: Center for Excellence in Service, Center for Electronic Markets and Enterprises, Supply Chain Management Center, Center for Human Capital, Innovation and Technology, Dingman Center for Entrepreneurship, Center for Health Information and Decision Systems, and Center for Global Business. The Smith School also houses about twenty clubs focusing on such special interest areas as marketing, finance, logistics, information technology, and international business. There are also a series of teaching and research laboratories for finance, supply chain management, behavioral research, and electronic markets.

Some of the school's units have exceptional special activities for students such as our Logistics Department and Logistics Club that conducts an annual Industry Day. Our Finance Department began an Undergraduate Finance Case Competition in 2003/2004. This case competition is linked to one of the department's finance courses and funded for a three-year period by an external donor.

Our Financial Markets Laboratory has engaged a group of about 15 undergraduate interns as part of the Campus' University Research Assistant Program (URAP). This student intern model, which has been very successful in the Finance Laboratory, will be extended to other laboratories such as the Supply Chain and Behavioral Research Labs. Each area and research center within the Smith School will be tasked to design one or more focused experience to highlight its business segment specifically and to maximize the undergraduate experience. For example, in the fall of 2006, the finance department will launch an undergraduate investment fund, similar in operation to the very successful MBA Mayer Fund, in which undergraduates will manage real money and report to real donors. Similarly, the Financial Markets Lab will continue offering a unique financial certification program in Reuters 3000Xtra, the only Reuters financial certification program offered in any business school in the world.

Plans are underway to introduce two new Smith Fellows Tracks in marketing. The first, "Computational Marketing," is a unique venture between our Marketing and Decision and Information Technologies Departments. This program derives from the tremendous acceleration of computational technologies, the rapid explosion of marketplace data from both the consumers and producers' sides, and the pervasiveness of intelligence driven decision making. Currently, it is the only such undergraduate program of its kind. The Marketing Department is also launching an E-Fellows track. The Logistics, Business and Public Policy Department will begin a specially devised Supply Chain Fellows Program and the Accounting and Information Assurance Department is planning two fellows programs.

Other program ideas under development include:

- Sports Management   - Real Estate
- Leadership   - Business and the Arts
- Consulting   - Philanthropy and Not-For-Profits

Courtesy of Howard Frank, the University of Maryland

APPENDIX D

ANNUAL SCORECARD

Performance Measures	2001	2002	2003	2004	2005

Student Placement:

Average Salary
    MBA
    MAcc
    Undergraduate

% of Students with Offers at Graduation
    MBA
    MAcc
    Undergraduate

Three months after graduation
    MBA
    MAcc
    Undergraduate

Placement of Doctoral Students
    Domestic Doctoral Granting
    Domestic Non-Doctoral Granting
    International

Teaching:

Percentage of Classes Taught by:
    Tenure Track Faculty
    Instructors
    Adjuncts
    GTFs

Average Percentage of Class Rating Teaching as Good or Very Good
    Tenure Track Faculty
    Instructors
    Adjuncts/Visitors
    GTFs

Students:

Average GPA of Entering Students
    Undergraduate
    MBA
    MAcc

Average GMAT Score of Entering Students
    MBA
    MAcc
    Ph.D.

Funding:

    Pre-business
    Minor
    Undergraduate Major
    Graduate
    Other
    Total
    Donations (by school year)
    (Broken out by purpose and cash flows and pledges at later date)

Recognition:

References in Media
    National
    Regional

Presentations
    Conferences
    Community

Diversity:

Percentage of Women
    Tenure Track Faculty & Instructors
    Invited to Campus on Recruiting Trips

Percentage of Minorities
    Tenure Track Faculty & Instructors
    Invited to Campus on Recruiting Trips

Percentage of Women Students Entering
    Undergraduate
    Masters
    Ph.D.

Percentage of Minority Students Entering
    Undergraduate
    Masters
    Ph.D.

Percentage of International Students Entering
    Undergraduate
    Masters
    Ph.D.

Courtesy of James C. Bean, the University of Oregon

APPENDIX E

STUDENT EXIT SURVEY

UPPER DIVISION CORE

1.   To what extent did you take business courses in the recommended sequence?

2.   Thinking about the upper division core (Mgmt 321, BA 352, BE 325, Fin 311, Fin 316, Mktg 311, DSc 330, DSc 335, DSc 340, BA 453) to what extent was there unnecessary duplication of content?

3.   How satisfied were you with the availability of upper division courses?

4.   How satisfied were you with the average size of your upper division core courses?

5.   How would you rate the quality of teaching in the upper division core courses?

6.   Are you a student in the LCB Honors Program?

7.   Are you a transfer student?

8.   Are you an Accounting major? (If no, skip to question 14)

9.   To what extent was there unproductive duplication in the set of courses in your accounting sequence?

10.   In what area(s), specifically, did you find duplication?

11.   How satisfied were you with the availability of courses in your accounting major?

12.   How satisfied were you with the average size of your accounting courses?

13. How would you rate the quality of teaching in your accounting courses?

ELECTIVES

14. If you are a BADM major, what is your concentration? (If accounting major, skip to question 26)

   a. _____ entrepreneurship

   b. _____ finance

   c. _____ information systems and operations management

   d. _____ marketing

   e. _____ sports business

   f. _____ general business

15. To what extent was there unproductive duplication in the set of courses in your concentration?

16. In what area(s), specifically, did you find duplication?

17. How satisfied were you with the availability of courses in your concentration?

18. How satisfied were you with the average size of your concentration courses?

19. How would you rate the quality of teaching in your concentration courses?

20. For those with more than one concentration (if not, skip to question 26), what was your second concentration?

   a. _____ entrepreneurship

   b. _____ finance

c.   _____ information systems and operations management

d.   _____ marketing

e.   _____ sports business

21.   To what extent was there unproductive duplication in the set of courses in your second concentration?

22.   In what area(s), specifically, did you find duplication?

23.   How satisfied were you with the availability of courses in your second concentration?

24.   How satisfied were you with the average size of your second concentration courses?

25.   How would you rate the quality of teaching in your second concentration courses?

OVERALL LCB EXPERIENCE

26.   How satisfied were you with your LCB instructors relating concepts to the real world?

27.   To what extent do you feel the business school has prepared you to make difficult ethical decisions you'll be facing in business?

28.   To what extent do you feel the business school has prepared you to address social responsibility issues you might face?

29.   How satisfied were you with the opportunities for practical experiences within the undergraduate curriculum?

30.   How active were you in club(s) or organization (s) within the Lundquist College and how satisfied were you with the activities provided by the club or organization?

a. American Marketing Association

b. Alpha Kappa Psi

c. Beta Alpha Psi

d Entrepreneur Club

e. UO Finance Association

f. UO Investment Group

g. Toastmasters

h. Sustainable Business Group

i. Warsaw Sports Business Club

j. Women in Business

31. What would have allowed you or encouraged you to participate more in clubs or organizations?

32. How satisfied were you with the training to improve presentation skills?

33. How satisfied were you with the training to improve writing skills?

34. How satisfied were you with the training to work effectively in teams?

35. How satisfied were you with the ability of your fellow students to work in teams?

36. Thinking about the team experiences you've had in the Lundquist College, approximately how many team projects did you participate in? How many did you find valuable? How many did you find of little value?

37. How satisfied were you with LCB Career Services' assistance in helping you to develop your job search skills/tools and to understand the search process for career opportunities?

38. What sources did you use to learn about career opportunities (check all that apply)?

____ Email Newsletter Postings – LCB Career Services

____ Email Career Newsletter/Job Postings – UO Career Center

____ Faculty Referral

____ Campus Interview Program (Employer Interviews on Campus)

____ Employer Presentation on Campus

____ Personal Networking, Informational Interviewing

____ Previous summer or Internship Employer

____ Internet Searching

____ Targeted Letter Writing

____ Responding to Advertisement (online, newspaper, etc.)

39. How satisfied were you with the number and variety of companies and full-time career opportunities presented to you via campus sources?

40. How satisfied were you with your access to Lundquist College alumni in cultivating career opportunities?

41. How frequently did you use LCB professional advisors, LCB peer advisors, LCB group advising session? (At least once/term, once/year, never. If never, please indicate what kept you from using advising services.

42. How satisfied were you with the quality of advising you obtained in the Lundquist College of Business. Please explain your answer.

43. How often did you read the communications from the Lundquist College of Business advising office (rarely, often......etc.)

44. Did you participate in an overseas study program while in college?

    a.   Yes (indicate where): _____

b.   No: _____

c.   Please indicate what best describes why you didn't study overseas

    i.   Not interested

    ii.   Money

    iii.   Would cause a delay in graduation

    iv.   Didn't know I could study overseas

    v.   Language skills

    vi.   Other _____

45.   How satisfied were you with the academic quality of your fellow business students?

46.   How satisfied were you with the level of camaraderie (i.e. friendly good fellowship) that was present in your business school student body?

47.   Rate the value of the investment you made in your undergraduate business degree.

48.   How inclined are you to recommend your Lundquist College undergraduate business degree to a close friend?

49.   Which professor at the Lundquist College of Business has influenced you the most?

50.   What is the one thing you would change to improve the Lundquist College of Business?

Courtesy of James C. Bean, the University of Oregon

APPENDIX F

VISION AND MISSION

Lundquist College of Business

University of Oregon

July, 2006

Vision:

The Lundquist College will be internationally renowned for excellence in business education and research drawing strength from its links to Pacific Rim neighbors and distinctive qualities of Oregon culture: innovation, sustainability, active lifestyles, financial stewardship, and respect for individuality and diversity within an increasingly global community.

Mission:

The Lundquist College is an integral part of the state's flagship AAU university, which is a liberal arts, public, research institution. The College's mission is to:

1.   Provide outstanding undergraduate education that combines a strong foundation in the liberal arts, excellence in traditional business disciplines and experiential opportunities drawing on the strength of Oregon's distinctive qualities.

2.   Support economic development by offering master's programs associated with signature centers derived from Oregon's distinctive qualities, and by providing expert services to the Oregon community and beyond.

3.   Contribute to the advancement of business knowledge through scholarship and doctoral programs in accordance with the research mission of the university.

Strategy

We implement this mission via disciplinary research and education in accounting, decision sciences, finance, management, and marketing combined with experiential education and interdisciplinary research in our signature themes of entrepreneurship/innovation, securities analysis, sports business, and sustainable supply chain management. Transition from disciplinary to experiential education is supported by leadership education focused on communication, teamwork, ethics, and personal leadership development. The disciplines are organized by departments and governed by an academic council. The signature themes and leadership are organized by centers and governed by a professional council.

Courtesy of James C. Bean, the University of Oregon

APPENDIX G

MISSION STATEMENT, SHARED VALUES, AND GOALS

James Madison University Mission Statement

We are committed to preparing students to be educated and enlightened citizens who will lead productive and meaningful lives.

College of Business Mission Statement

The College of Business is committed to preparing students to be active and engaged citizens who are exceptionally well qualified leaders for success in a global competitive marketplace.

Shared Values and Goals

- The JMU CoB aspires to be among the top ten percent of undergraduate business programs in the nation, striving for excellence and continuous improvement in undergraduate learning. Its student body comes primarily from the Mid-Atlantic region of the United States and, to a growing extent, from the Northeast.

- Directed toward a full-time, traditional-age student population, the CoB's undergraduate programs are based on solid foundations in general education and an integrated business core curriculum. Beyond these foundations, the CoB offers students a wide variety of programs that emphasize theory, application, and experiential learning in a business discipline.

- CoB faculty are committed to providing an exceptional educational experience for students, with an emphasis on developing leadership, technology, communication and integrative skills.

- The CoB will be a preferred source of student talent for employers in the Mid-Atlantic region.

- The CoB takes an entrepreneurial approach to graduate programs, developing niche programs for which there is a need and for which the faculty has competence.

- Student learning is assessed frequently. Assurance of learning programs are designed to assess learning in the business core, each of the undergraduate majors, and each of the degree programs within the CoB. Consistent with academic freedom, faculty members are encouraged to take an active role in innovative curriculum development and assessment processes designed to improve the educational experience.

- The CoB recognizes that students and faculty face ethical choices. As such, it maintains the highest expectations for students regarding JMU's Honor Code. Furthermore, the CoB, strives to prepare students for the ethical tensions and dilemmas they will face in the course of their professional lives. Additionally, the CoB demands the utmost in professional and ethical conduct by its faculty towards students, the community of scholars, and society at large.

- CoB faculty members believe that a balance between teaching and research is the most effective way to educate their students. Scholarly contributions complement classroom teaching by helping faculty members maintain currency in their discipline. Furthermore, students gain a deeper understanding of subject matter, a greater appreciation of a discipline's body of knowledge, and added enthusiasm for learning when they are taught by active scholars.

- Faculty members are committed to a broad array of intellectual pursuits and scholarly output in discipline-based scholarship, contributions to practice, and learning and pedagogical research. The relative emphasis on these three areas will vary from one faculty member to another depending upon education, experience, and interests, but the pursuit of knowledge in each area will be used to enhance students' learning experiences.

Courtesy of Robert D. Reid, James Madison University

Management Best Sellers

Other Best Sellers

The Raising Venture Capital Collection
Published by Aspatore

▶**Pitching to Venture Capitalists** - Essential Strategies for Approaching VCs, Making Presentations, Entering Into Negotiations and Securing Funding - Written by Leading VC Patrick Ennis - $49.95

▶**Raising Capital for Entrepreneurs** - Industry Insiders on Angel Funding, Venture Capital, & Growth Money from Private Investors - – Includes Highlights on Advantages and Disadvantages of Each - $49.95

▶**Term Sheets & Valuations** - Best Selling Venture Capital Book of 2005 - Line by Line Descriptions of Each Clause and Negotiation Points - $14.95

▶**Deal Terms** - The Finer Points of Venture Capital Deal Structures, Valuations, Stock Options and Getting Deals Done (Wilmerding's Follow on Book to Term Sheets & Valuations and the Current Second Best Selling Venture Capital Book) - $49.95

▶**Venture Debt Alternatives and Evaluation Guidelines** - A Comprehensive Look at the Venture Debt Marketplace Along With a Systematic Framework for Approaching the Debt Capital Markets, Increasing Transaction Transparency and Avoiding Common, Costly Mistakes - - An Option Every Entrepreneur Should Consider in Addition to Venture Capital - $249.95

▶**Venture Capital Best Practices** - Leading VCs & Lawyers Keys to Success in Doing Venture Capital Deals - $49.95

▶**Compensation Structures for Venture Backed Companies** - How VCs Want to See the Structure of Management & Employee Compensation, Stock Options, Retirement, Debt & Bonus Plans - $119.95

▶**The Role of Board Members in Venture Backed Companies** - Rules, Responsibilities and Motivations of Board Members - From Management & VC Perspectives - $99.95

▶**Venture Capital Valuations** - Top VCs on Step-by-Step Strategies and Methodologies for Valuing Companies at All Stages - $99.95

▶**The Venture Capital Legal Handbook** - Industry Insiders on the Laws and Documents that Govern VC Deals, Raising Capital, M&A and More - Includes Every Major Document Used in VC Deals With Analysis & Negotiation Points - Save Thousands in Legal Fees - 820 Pages - $299.95

<u>Buy All 10 Titles Above – Save 40%</u>
(The Equivalent of 4 Books for Free) - $999.95
Call 1-866-Aspatore (277-2867) – Phone Order Rate Only

<u>Buy All 10 Titles Above Plus The CD-Rom of VC Documents & VC Financial Modeling</u> -
Save $1,000 (The Equivalent of All 10 Books for Free) - $1,999.95